Lights Out

Lights Out

A Cuban Memoir of Betrayal and Survival

DANIA ROSA NASCA

ISBN-13: 9781537036052
ISBN-10: 153703605X
Library of Congress Control Number: 2016913352
CreateSpace Independent Publishing Platform
North Charleston, South Carolina

Dedication

In memory of my parents and all our dearly departed from the past.
To my son, Anthony, as his legacy to take into the future.

Contents

Preface

This memoir is not intended to be a history book, but it is not fiction either. The events described happened in Cuba before Fidel Castro came into power and during the early years of Castro's regime. They are the experiences of my elders, who experienced the revolution as adults, and my own experiences of it as a child.

Lights Out is a story of love and betrayal, the birth and death of a republic, the flaming up and the snuffing out of the torch of liberty that burns so brightly in every human heart. When Fidel took over Cuba, the lights, figuratively and literally, were extinguished.

This memoir will inform those who are curious about what Cuba and the Cuban people were really like before Fidel, Che Guevara, and the Cuban Revolution; its aftermath; and the chain of events that led to Fidel's rise to power. There is a certain intrigue attached to revolution in Cuba, with its images of bearded guerillas fighting from the mountains for a beautiful tropical island and the freedom of its people. Yet, as I point out, except for the first heady days of the Cuban Revolution in

1959, Cuban society soon began to show the inexorable signs of totalitarian takeover. Our heartfelt revolution for freedom was stolen from us.

There is an old joke that if the communists took over the Sahara Desert, there would soon be a shortage of sand. I lived through the shortages that befell Cuba, inexorably, like the closing of the proverbial iron curtain, on a previously prosperous society as communism was instituted. In addition to the loss of religious and basic freedoms, in Fidel's Cuba there were no longer shoes for children, medicines for the sick, safe infrastructure, or replacements for mechanical parts when something as simple as an electric fan broke down in the sweltering tropical heat.

Those who have read *Animal Farm* or other accounts of communist takeovers will recognize my story. In communist societies, neighbors spy on neighbors; people disappear to prison camps for minor infractions or imagined ones; the government seeks to control the very minds of its citizens; the centrally planned, government-dictated economy strangles itself, leaving shortages of almost everything; and the human spirit of innovation, entrepreneurship, creativity, generosity, and reverence is systematically stifled.

Fidel sold out our cherished national hopes, accomplishments, and dreams. He gave Cuba, body and soul, to the Soviet Union in exchange for his own power. Our vibrant nation became a communist satellite, a soulless entity whose colorful, diverse, and passionate national identity was deliberately snuffed out.

It wasn't until many years later, when I began to do research, that I became informed about the true political, economic, and social history of Cuba. Fidel's goal to create a new communist generation included expunging much of Cuban history from schools and libraries. There were book burnings. What was not burned was rewritten and distorted to serve the government's purposes. My investigation also revealed the chain of events that led to Fidel's rise to power.

Knowing my country's real history filled me with a stronger sense of regret and also a fierce and loving pride. The aspirations of a conscientious and freedom-loving people were stolen away. They did not deserve the inhuman system that was imposed on them to crush them. Cubans were a people who seemed naturally gifted for democracy with their strong sense of self-determination. They were also a humane and genteel people.

There is no substitute for testimony from the survivors of any brutal totalitarian government. The survivors lived it, and their stories should be heeded.

Yet I often feel that Cubans who have lived through and survived Fidel's brutalities have been unduly silenced, as if our living experiences were somehow invalid because they don't fit the popular narrative about Cuba. Many people, Americans among them, have erroneously cast Fidel and Che as heroes. They believe that the Cuban Revolution was a class war and that Fidel ousted Fulgencio Batista, when in reality, Batista was ousted by a *whole nation* yearning to be free. Fidel simply *filled a vacuum* of leadership and then co-opted the revolution for communism.

Apologists for Fidel's cruel regime have ignorantly or maliciously portrayed the Cuban middle class as callous rich people, despite the fact that lower- to upper-middle-class Cubans earned incomes with hard work and entrepreneurship, just as North Americans have always done.

The names of many people have been omitted or limited to first names in this memoir because inclusion of full names could endanger or be problematic for the individual or the individual's family. All uncited information that did not come from my own memory or from widely distributed news reports came from these anonymous Cuban sources. I have withheld their names to protect them.

* * *

Before Fidel, the world baptized Cuba as the Pearl of the Caribbean. Like an oyster that sacrifices its life to give birth to a perfect pearl, Cuba sacrificed much. It shed blood, not once, not twice, but three times—the Little War (1879–1880), Ten Years' War (1868–1878), and Cuban War of Independence (1895–1898)—to gain independence from Spain and to establish a constitutional republic. The final three months of the conflict escalated to become the Spanish–American War.

Nuzzled by the Gulf of Mexico and the Caribbean Sea, the island of Cuba seemed destined to prosper, even under the rule of the Spaniards. It had fertile soil and favorable weather, very much like that of Mediterranean Spain.

Spanish cattle ranchers planted sugar cane and erected sugar mills. Cuba's sugar industry was boosted by a brief British occupation in the late 1700s that forced Spain to lift trade restrictions, as well as a slave rebellion that disrupted Haiti's sugar production.[1] Soon Cuban sugar and tobacco were recognized as the best in the world.

Thousands of small and productive sugar, coffee, and tobacco farms were created when Spain granted land to farmers who had occupied it for some time. By 1860, the island had approximately two thousand sugar mills.[2]

Besides being fertile and productive, Cuba was beautiful. Spanish colonization gave birth to exquisite colonial architecture, much like that of Granada and Toledo.

Most of the people who came to Cuba wanted to stay, and many did. Very poor Spaniards, many from the Spanish Canary Islands, came to Cuba—as did three of my great-grandparents—looking for work and a better life. They found it.

Until the mid-1950s, when civil unrest began, Cuba was a multiracial, integrated haven. Spaniards, Chinese, Europeans, English, Eastern Europeans, Russian Jews, and Middle Eastern nationals all immigrated to Cuba in the early twentieth century to escape persecution or turmoil in their homelands. Others who were sailing to the United States via Cuba ended up choosing the beautiful and friendly island as their home.

Some Cubans arrived unwillingly as African slaves. Most were baptized, and many of them were educated while still slaves. Later many became *mambises** and fought with other Cubans in the Ten Years' War of 1868–1878, after which slavery was abolished. After a period of transition from slavery

---

* Cuban guerilla fighters.

to freedom, called the period of *patronato* (tutelage),[*] blacks became part of society. Cuba was a society that valued hard work. Anyone who was willing to work hard could get ahead, regardless of skin color or ethnicity, and enjoy respect and belonging.

Many Haitian slaves came to Cuba after Haiti was liberated from France. White Frenchmen and women who did not want to go back to France also came to Cuba. These immigrants settled mostly in Santiago, becoming successful and productive, and they too became Cubans. Regardless of your race or economic status, when you came to Cuba, you were Cuban. Thus, Cuba became the second melting pot of the world.

After four hundred years of Spanish domination, as well as invasions by the French and English, Cubans wanted their freedom. Although appreciative of their mother country, Spain, they began fighting for their independence.

Spain's inhumane treatment of many poor Cubans gave the United States a reason to insert itself into Cuba's struggle for independence in 1898. In my opinion, everyone in the region benefited from this intervention, with Cuba being the biggest beneficiary. In addition to the obvious benefits of self-governance, the birth of the republic opened the door to better conditions for Cuba's poor, for Cuba had access to new world markets, which included the United States and other countries.

Nonetheless, U.S. intervention in the war was painful for some Cubans because the great Cuban heroes who had fought the Spaniards for many years were kept from participating

---

[*] http://www.historyofcuba.com/history/race/EndSlave.htm.

in the 1898 treaty with Spain. The reasons are uncertain, but the exclusion was insulting. Although most Cubans were not offended, many Cubans obsessed about the idea of American imperialism and were quick to become bitter toward the United States. This resentment was handed down to later generations.

The U.S. military temporarily stayed in Cuba to maintain order and to protect Cuba from falling back into Spanish hands. From that moment on, until the arrival of Fidel's anti-American propaganda, Cubans and Americans for the most part enjoyed a sincere, mutual friendship.

The island became the new Republic of Cuba. Almost all residents automatically became Cuban citizens. My paternal and maternal grandparents—children of three *Isleños**and one *Sevillano†*—were born toward the end of the War of Independence. Initially they were citizens of Spain and subjects of the Spanish king. Soon after their birth, they became sons and daughters of a republic.

In 1902, Cubans wrote and adopted their first constitution and elected Tomás Estrada Palma to be the first president. The United States then pulled out of Cuba. Before leaving, under the Platt Amendment and with the agreement of both republics, the United States acquired 36,000 acres of land on Guantánamo Bay and was granted the right to intervene in Cuba to preserve order and protect the liberty, property, and life of Cubans. Only the prideful or foolish would not have welcomed such a friend.

---

* Natives of the Canary Islands, which are located off the coast of Africa and most of which are Spanish provinces.

† Native of Sevilla, Spain.

In 1934, Franklin Roosevelt's New Deal stipulated that although the military base at Guantánamo Bay remained U.S. territory, the United States could no longer intervene in Cuban affairs. Little did Cubans know how advantageous this change in Cuban–American relations would be to Fidel thirty years later.

Republican Cuba wasn't perfect, but it is factual to say that Cuba before Fidel was neither economically nor socially backward. Based on commonly used indicators, its standard of living was the third highest in the region. That was no small feat for a young republic. Many outside Cuba saw Cuba as a glass half empty, but before Fidel, most Cubans saw Cuba as a glass half full.

Much has been made of Batista and the Cuban casinos. El Tropicana was one of the few casinos in Cuba before Batista came into power. During his regime, casinos connected to the American mafia started popping up, mostly in Havana. These fueled the misconception that Cuba was under U.S. criminal control. Yes, there were casinos and, yes, some were controlled by criminal elements, but all of this has been overstated. Cubans were not forced to patronize these casinos, and the casinos had little impact on Cuban life.

Many observers of Cuba seem to be obsessed with the idea of the Cuban peasant before Fidel. It is important to note that there was a big difference between European and Russian peasants and the Cuban peasant. The European or Russian peasant was a serf working for a landlord in a feudal society. In the Republic of Cuba, Cuban peasants were self-maintaining men who worked and progressed according to their ability. Some Cuban peasants worked the land; others worked in rural industries, such as textile mills. Wherever they worked, they were paid employees. As in any other country, some jobs paid better than others, and there were different levels of economic achievement. However, industries and unions were strong in rural Cuba, sugar workers were well paid, and not all rural families were poor.

Some peasants were educated, and many Cuban peasants became landowners and prospered while, as noted, others remained poor for a variety of reasons. Additionally, just as the term "rich" is a relative term, so is the term "poor." Many Cubans of very modest means, whom Americans might consider poor, made up what Cubans referred to as the lower middle class. Cubans had a lot of pride. If they could afford rent and food and had a Sunday-best outfit, they did not see themselves as poor.

It is also a myth that all country homes in Cuba were pitiful thatched huts with dirt floors. Many farmers had well-built farmhouses. Even in humble homes with dirt floors, which were sprinkled daily to maintain a smooth, hard surface, I never saw a messy, dirty house. People took great pride in their homes and in themselves.

Whether they lived in a big house or a humble *bohio*,* rural Cubans, like all Cubans, enjoyed their freedom. Even the poor know when liberty is taken from them.

Many *campesinos* came to the big cities to get ahead. People from outlying areas piled into makeshift tin dwellings with palm branches for roofs. Dreams and hope were alive, though; a better life was attainable. Before Fidel came into power, the

---

* Hut.

employment that was available to Cubans, either working for others or in one's own business, was not the pseudowork of the communist slogan, "Everyone has a job." Real work existed that allowed workers to earn a living. Additionally, Cubans had freedom to spend their money as they wished.

My maternal grandparents were *colonos*[*] who grew sugar cane and were part of a group of landowners who were contracted with a *central*[†] to sell their sugar cane. All of the *colonias*[‡] were near the railroad track. The *colonos* would bring their ox or horse carts loaded with sugar cane to the railroad, which would then carry the cane to the central market. After the harvest was sold, the farmers received payment. From beginning to end, the sugar industry in Cuba was the most organized and most profitable of all of the country's industries.

My grandfather owned some land, wagons, horses, and an ox. His farm was the family's modest source of income, and it provided the stake for him to start building houses in Holguín. Later, after my grandparents moved to Holguín, and before Fidel's agrarian "reform" stripped them of their land, the farm continued to help support my grandparents, their two unmarried adult daughters, and my uncle.

Like all farmers, my grandparents had chickens, pigs, and plenty of food. They were literate and knew their math because they had attended one-room country schools. They were

---

[*] Owners of a colonia. (See footnote **.)

[†] Sugar mill.

[‡] Sugar plantations/farms. This term was used regardless of how big or small the parcel of land was.

married in and followed the Catholic faith. They lived in a sturdy *casa de campo*[*] constructed of wood and supported by strong tree logs. The family had no luxuries beyond the basics. They never owned a car.

Family ties were very strong; aunts and uncles were like second parents, and cousins were like brothers and sisters. The Bible was read every day, and children had great respect for their elders. If an adult entered a room, a child automatically got up and offered his or her seat. Dads worked the land, moms took care of the children, and children took care of the animals.

My grandfather was a tall, slim man who with great ease could do math both on paper and in his head. He tilled the rich soil with an ox plow and hired seasonal sugar-industry workers to help him. The ox had to be allowed to rest in the shade and given plenty of water to avoid heatstroke, especially when the heat and sun were intense between noon and two o'clock. Then it was time to go home for lunch and *la siesta*,[†] which allowed not only the farmer but also the ox to rest and cool off.

As a child, I loved hearing the stories my mom told me about growing up on the farm. She had dolls made of corn-husks, and she lovingly made dresses for them from flour sacks and leftover fabric. She wished for a store-bought doll, but in those days, children were brought up to have their needs

---

[*] Farmhouse.

[†] Midday rest.

met—not their wants. *Papasito,*[*] as we affectionately called my grandfather, was caring and generous, and he surely would have bought my mother a doll had she asked. Instead of asking, my mom promised herself that if she ever had a daughter, she would buy her a doll.

She remembers Dr. Pérez Zorrilla, one of Holguín's first doctors, visiting the country once a week, riding on a horse. Medical care was available in many rural areas, provided by doctors who traveled from a city to *el campo* to care for the *campesinos.*[†] So much for those who believe Fidel brought medicine and health care to Cuba.

In the Cuba before Castro and as far back as colonial times, dreams could be achieved. Life wasn't easy, but there was hope, and hope nourished dreams, which with work could be fulfilled.

Before Fidel, Cuba belonged to the Cuban people. In 1958, 62 percent of the sugar mills were owned by Cubans, and only 14 percent of the capital invested in the island came from the United States.[3] With the exception of a few U.S. companies and some other foreign businesses, which were mostly in Havana, almost all businesses in Cuba's cities and towns were family owned. U.S. products played a vibrant role in the economy, but Cuba *never* belonged to the United States or to any other country. The productive, industrious, and successful Cuban people created their own robust economy, with more than fifty thousand small and medium-sized family owned businesses.[4]

---

[*] Affectionate diminutive of Papa.

[†] Rural people.

In 1948, the same year President Prío took office, my mother became a young bride of twenty, marrying my father in Holguín in June. My parents went to Havana for their honeymoon. There were dozens of hotels in Havana for all income levels. Some were big and fancy; some smaller and family owned. The young couple didn't have a lot of money, but Havana, an enchanting place, had a way of making both Cubans and foreigners feel carefree and happy. Just sightseeing, going to the famous department store El Encanto,* and walking along El Malecón† made the couple happy.

The newlyweds returned to Holguín to begin their shared life in a rented apartment. By then my father was working in Holguín's main bakery on Calle Cervantes.

Postwar prosperity did not completely eliminate poverty in Cuba; there were Cubans of all races who were still poor and lived on twenty-five cents a day in rural areas. Some lived in regions that were less productive than others, and they couldn't or wouldn't move. Some were plagued by social or self-inflicted misery, others were plain lazy, and yet others were content with the life they led and did not aspire to do more.

Like any young republic, Cuba needed to mature. It had some setbacks, but it always bounced back. When Fidel stole the revolution, turning it into something its original leaders never intended it to be, time stood still. Everything that was not destroyed stagnated. There was no bouncing back. The Cuba of

---

* The Enchantment.

† A broad esplanade, roadway, and seawall that stretches for eight kilometers along the coast in Havana.

today is an altered Cuba, decimated in every way—economically, physically, and spiritually. It bears no resemblance to its former illustrious self.

The Cuban people longed for freedom from the Batista regime and bought it with their blood and bones, only to have their victory co-opted by a soulless and rigid ideology: the Marxist–Leninist ideology of 1917. Thus, a promising and beautiful country, the Pearl of the Caribbean, was shattered, as was the dream of self-determination, of dignity, and of a prosperous future, a dream that had been cherished in Cuban hearts for a very long time.

The United States left a constitutional, democratic republic that was on a roll of prosperity. The Cuban people met and conquered the challenges of each decade. By 1958, the year before Fidel seized power, and the year I was born, Cuba not only had the third-highest standard of living in the region, but it also had a low unemployment rate of 7 percent[5] and ranked seventh and eighth highest in the world for agricultural and industrial salaries, respectively.[6]

When I left Cuba in 1970, I left a starving country on its way to bankruptcy because of Fidel's Stalin-style, communist dictatorship. The Pearl of the Caribbean was no more.

A Vignette

There Used to Be a Carousel

Every year a traveling fair, Los Caballitos (the Little Horses) de Labrada, came to the town where I was born and raised: Holguín, Cuba. The fair came to the same spot every year: an empty, dusty field on the corner of Calles Fomento and Aricochea. It was a simple but colorful traveling amusement park, and it brought much joy to children and parents alike. The fair had all kinds of rides, but the carousel with its horses was the most beloved.

Anticipation of Los Caballitos was a wonderful feeling for me. Each year I was bubbling over with excitement, remembering the beautiful carousel, the music, the different food vendors, and the admission tickets that cost just pennies. It was there that I first tasted cotton candy. I remember my parents' delight when they first introduced me to it. I still remember my amazement when the vendor kept turning the stick around and around, and the cotton candy grew bigger and bigger. When I finally tasted it, I could not believe how quickly or how sweetly it dissolved on my tongue.

Although the government takeover of large private businesses was spreading to medium-sized and some smaller businesses at the time, Los Caballitos de Labrada was still operating freely, or so it appeared. Yet the last time Los Caballitos came to town, it brought a different experience. For me, it was the most powerful realization of how everything that was colorful, joyful, and beautiful had disappeared or turned gray.

I was so excited when I saw the workers setting up the rides. Finally, the day came. I was going to go on the carousel first. I got a couple of coins from my mother and ran as fast as I could to the lot.

Arriving, I stopped dead in my tracks. My feet froze to the ground. I felt as if a giant with a huge hand had slapped me across the face and stopped my heart.

There in front of me was the carousel, except it didn't have its beautiful, multicolored horses and carriages, its organ, and its sprightly music. The beautiful, bright horses were gone, replaced by flat, wooden cutouts in the shape of horses that were held together with screws or glue and painted an ugly, dark, uniform gray.

If there were any other rides, I did not notice. The place was deserted. There was no music, excitement, or joy. One look at the carousel was all I needed to see. I turned around and went home, my heart and stomach aching with an enormous sadness. I can only describe it as a sickened feeling throughout my body and permeating my being; it was that dark, gray, and depressing. *Everything, absolutely everything, is gone or gray, gray, gray.* This thought ran over and over again in my mind. I was ten years old.

Eventually, Los Caballitos de Labrada would be closed by the government, but not before it came to towns all over Cuba one last time: gray, ugly, and lifeless, to shatter the heart of every child.

Only those of us who lived under Fidel know that the travesty must have been calculated. I remember thinking, *My God, there will be nothing, nothing to look forward to*, and that was the purpose. It was part of the soulless implementation of the communist state's plan to rob children of joy, dreams, and childhood; to mold them into spiritless communists. Castro stole happiness from children and from their parents.

Sometimes I think Fidel stole more from the poor than from the rich, for the arrival of Los Caballitos gave even the most impoverished children a moment in the sunshine each year. Even the poorest could scrape together the few pennies to ride the carousel and experience the delight, freedom, and flights of fancy children need to nourish their imaginations. We were robbed of even that precious beam of sunlight in our child lives. It was done to extinguish the light in our souls.

*Man loves liberty, even if he does
not know that he loves it.
He is driven by it and flees from
where it does not exist.*

José Martí

One

Judas Goat and the Milk Bottle

The government was invading our very teeth and bones. It dictated what we could eat and drink. Milk was prohibited, even for children.

My father had developed an ulcer, so he qualified for a daily bottle of government-issued, watered-down milk. Can you imagine needing a doctor's note to buy a bottle of milk?

Each evening, someone from my family would take the empty bottle over to my grandmother's house, and my aunt or uncle would go the next morning to a government-owned store to get it refilled.

One evening my mother held the bottle out to me and said, "We forgot to take the milk bottle over to Grandma's."

"It's getting dark. Why do I have to go?" I complained.

---

* Beginning with 1960, Castro named each year with a slogan.

1

"You are almost twelve. You'll be fine. Now hurry."

I grudgingly took the milk bottle and set off. The round-trip walk would not take more than five minutes. Even though the tentacles of government were intruding into virtually every aspect of our lives, it was safe for an eleven-year-old to walk such a short distance alone. Our neighbors' families had known one another for generations and were interwoven with one another's lives. The children all played together and grew up side by side, going to one another's parties; the adults knew each child by name, age, and temperament. Everyone looked out for everyone else. It was a close-knit community. So why was I feeling so apprehensive? I scoped the neighborhood for signs of trouble.

I walked on the familiar sidewalk as if expecting it to crack beneath my feet. There was an iron anvil in the pit of my stomach. Before I turned right at the corner, I looked back to make sure my mom was watching me from our front door. She was. Slightly relieved, I went on, cradling the empty milk bottle to my bosom for comfort.

I couldn't help but enjoy the tropical night. Oh, those Cuban nights! The grace of sundown in burning climates brings an incomparable peace and a deep sigh of relief. The penetrating heat on the street was chastened by nightfall, although the air was still close and moist, like an embrace around my bare arms. The night—humid, clammy, and familiar—held in it the reassurance that tomorrow would be sunny again, and the next day, and the next. There were few people out at this time, and the nocturnal insects were just beginning to tune their instruments for the serenade I fell asleep to each night. They rattled and buzzed like tiny gourd instruments and tambourines. It was my Cuba still, in spite of everything.

I had not gone more than a few steps down this block when I saw him—a man lurking in the shadows of Carmita's doorstep. I almost gasped aloud. My instincts immediately told me why this man, his features becoming more recognizable by the second, was there. He had become a *chivato*, a secret police informant. Carmita had been the former *cheka** or chief of the Defense Committee for her block, and she had quit. Each block had a *cheka*. When someone had a problem, they were supposed to take it to the *cheka*.

In reality, the *cheka* was the first line of the communist state security system, and the *cheka's* real duties were to spy on and report on the neighbors. When Carmita learned the true role of the *cheka*, she refused to be a part of it.

It was 1969, and only those of us who lived through the implementation of Castro's regime knew how courageous this woman was. By 1969, if you were in the party system, you stayed in it for fear of retaliation from the government. Yet this brave neighbor had renounced her communist party post, and in further repudiation of the regime, she had applied to leave Cuba on the Freedom Flights. She had cooked her own goose, though, and the spy at her door proved that.

My legs turned to lead, yet I dared not turn and run. That would draw his attention, and he might run after me. I walked forward like an automaton, fighting to look unafraid. The light was just enough to reveal that he was leaning toward, almost

---

* A Russian word for supervisor or head.

brushing against, Carmita's closed front door. His right ear was all but pressed to the door. All I could hear from her home was the clinking and clanking of china dishes and pans being cleaned after dinner, but the dark and intense expression on his face as he strained to listen to the voices inside showed he thought he could catch more than the usual sounds of a family evening. He seemed to embody the fear that had such a grip on me this dusky night.

I was almost upon him, so leaving undetected was not an option. He turned fully toward me, facing me. I stopped breathing. Petrified, I also ceased walking. He immediately realized that I knew what he was doing.

"What are you doing here? It's getting dark, and you should not be out alone," he said. He inserted a caring, fatherly note into his voice.

"I am taking a milk bottle to my grandmother's," I managed to blurt out.

"Go on then," he instructed me, looking at the bottle I was clutching. "Hurry along."

Somehow I was able to move my feet, which felt like blocks of concrete. Then, once I got going, I walked faster than I had ever walked before. I dropped the bottle off without much talk, and then I raced back home at top speed, almost running past Carmita's house. Thank goodness by that time the *chivato* was nowhere to be seen.

I could not shake off the gripping fear of what this person had become. We called them Judas Goats, those of our own people who had sold their souls to the system and who betrayed us to the government for money and favors. A real

Judas Goat is a trained goat that leads sheep or other goats to the slaughter while its own life is spared. It is an apt description of these people.

I didn't tell anyone about the encounter. I was afraid that telling would endanger my own family and the family he was spying on, so I kept quiet. Had I told my mother, she would have found him and given him a piece of her mind, as she did with every snitch she discovered. In my mom's eyes, snitching on your fellow Cubans was a cardinal sin.

The whole affair left me with a bitter taste in my mouth. I realized that without the collusion of our own people, a totalitarian, communist system could not have succeeded in Cuba. Wherever there has been great injustice against humanity, it usually has been perpetrated by, or was with the collaboration of, a country's own citizens. When that happens, fear surrounds you on every side. You must censor your words; you must hide your thoughts. You become your own jailer to survive.

That night, as I lay in bed, I thought about how much life had changed for our family and for our fellow Cubans. Why was everything so tense and unpleasant, with threats of the unknown around every once familiar corner? I remember wondering how we had arrived at being so hungry and so unable to trust anyone, with neighbors betraying neighbors.

I remember thinking, *Dear God, what has led us to all this? Castro couldn't have just jumped out of nowhere to control our lives. How did Cuban life come to be like this? What happened?*

I knew that, deep inside, most Cubans were asking themselves the same tormented questions. Still, safety seemed to lie in silence and silence alone.

Two

THE ROARING TWENTIES

Cuba's most effective president, General Gerardo Machado, took office in 1925. When Machado came into office, Cuba was flowing in gold. The young republic was fragile and full of dreams. It was the biggest exporter of sugar in the world. More and more Cubans were prospering, and many were getting rich.

President Machado used the country's wealth well and had a very successful first term. Some people would even say it was a fantastic first term. Machado was a visionary. Although Cuba was already blessed with many state highways and a reliable railroad system, Machado connected all of Cuba internally by constructing a central highway to be funded by a gasoline tax. The new seven-hundred-mile Carretera Central* connected the island from Pinar del Río at the northwest tip to Oriente at the

---

* Central Highway.

southeast end. It was more than twenty feet wide and followed the backbone of the island, touching the coast only in three places: Havana, Matanzas, and Santiago de Cuba. To protect the pavement, farmers used service roads alongside, crossing the highway only at granite crossing points. According to a 1933 *Economic Geography* article, it was "a model of scientific construction, scenic beauty, and economic usefulness."

Indeed, it is one of the few pieces of infrastructure that has not succumbed to the nearly universal deterioration Cuba has suffered under Castro.

When finished, the Carretera Central opened the Republic of Cuba to new forms of prosperity.

Entrepreneurism burgeoned, as traveling salesmen were now easily able to supply small businesses on all parts of the island. Tourism increased as visitors brought their cars on the ferry from Florida to tour the whole island.

Among Machado's many other accomplishments were an impressive new capitol building and state-of the-art prison on Isla de Pinos, which featured rehabilitation programs such as farming. This was to become a prison where, after the revolution, Fidel incarcerated and tortured the brightest minds among the political prisoners.

Machado brought in American and European investors in an effort to diversify the Cuban economy. He promoted mining. Many people erroneously, unfairly, and deliberately portray Machado as a U.S. puppet. On the contrary, Machado did not want Cuba to be dependent on anyone. In fact, he promoted economic diversification to avoid such dependency. Foreign enterprises paid a special tax and made up a small percentage of the overall number of businesses. The Cuban republic, including most of its economy, belonged to the Cuban people.

During this prosperous time, while all of these exciting advancements were happening in Cuba, three births occurred in the young republic that would have profound and formative influences on my life.

My father, Mario Herrera, was born on August 16, 1925, outside the city of Holguín, Oriente. He was the oldest of four children in a family of very poor and humble people. Because my grandmother could read very little and could not write, she insisted all four of her children attend the free public schools that offered education to the eighth grade.

On May 31, 1928, my mother, Blanca Tejeda, was born to hardworking farmers on a *finca*[*] called El 25,[†] which was located outside Cacocún, a little way from Holguín, Oriente. She was the youngest of five children.

The third birth that made an indelible mark on my life occurred on August 13, 1926, when Fidel Alejandro Castro Ruz was born to a wealthy farming family in Birán, not too far from Holguín and Cacocún.

---

[*] Farm.

[†] The Twenty-Five.

My mother on left circa 1932, with cousins

My father, five years old

My parents, 1963

Three

In 1929, toward the end of his term, President Machado courted trouble. Because he had accomplished so much in his first term, the praise went to his head, and he thought either he was indispensable or his admirers convinced him so. Machado had Congress pass a law to extend his term of office and allow for the possibility of reelection. He then began to work with Congress to change the constitution to allow presidents to be elected for a second consecutive term.

Unrest brewed, and ill feelings toward Machado started almost immediately, especially among communist intellectuals in Havana's universities. Communists* have never been known for not taking advantage of any situation that will allow them to advance their ideology. They agitated Cuba almost from the birth of the republic. Intellectuals and youth, including uni-

---

* The Cuban Communist Party was founded in 1925.

versity students (who are often targeted by agitators) began brewing a revolution to oust Machado. In response, Machado resorted to some abuse of power to repress his political opponents. Although ill advised, Machado's crackdown did not affect the average Cuban, and the turmoil caused by his trying to extend his term of office did not affect the economy.

Then the U.S. stock market crashed in 1929, and the price of sugar plummeted. As a result, most mortgages on Cuban sugar mills were foreclosed. It was this event that caused some, *but only some*, of the big sugar mills to pass into the hands of the American corporations that were holding the mortgages.

The stock market crash, followed by global depression, helped precipitate Machado's downfall, clearing the way for a power-hungry army sergeant named Fulgencio Batista y Zaldivar, Castro's special nemesis.

In August 1933, Machado resigned and left Cuba. Later he was amnestied for extending his presidency, and in 1950, the Cuban Congress legitimized his second term. Machado did great things for Cuba.

Batista convinced the army to promote him to colonel and to oust Machado loyalists from the military. This allowed Batista to appoint military officers who were in his camp.

From 1933 until 1936, there was one president after another in Cuba. Some lasted only a few days. Batista was the strong man in charge. Yet the young republic's government continued to function. Congress approved and rejected new laws, and elected representatives who governed the republic according to the Cuban constitution. But there's no doubt Batista was in the background.

In the turbulent early thirties, my mother's parents decided to move to the city. They had saved money and purchased land on Calle Fomento.* My grandfather built a house on Fomento and moved his family into it. Later, after building several houses on Fomento, my grandparents moved to Calle Cervantes and gave one of the Fomento homes to my parents so that my family could live close by. This family home was my residence until I left Cuba at age twelve.

Our house shared features with the big colonial homes of the city. To mitigate the heat and the almost palpable humidity, the indoor ceilings were supported by giant wood beams at least twenty feet high. Our front door came right to the sidewalk, and the open-air front windows were covered with hand-forged wrought iron. On the inside, wood door-like panels could be opened fully or partially for ventilation.

My mom loved her street with special affection because of the role her father played in its development with his building, renting, and selling of houses. Among the houses he built were the two next to ours heading toward Calle Martí. These he kept as rentals.

I can just see my hardworking grandfather building all of these houses, hiring masons and carpenters, and doing much of the work himself. My grandfather helped build the Republic of Cuba! None of the houses he built were luxurious, but they were spacious, strong houses built to last and intended to serve many generations to come.

---

* Fomento Street, also known as Calle General Marrero.

The family was not wealthy, but they were comfortable. They, like other Cubans, could enjoy the fruits of their industriousness. Everyone saved their pennies for special occasions. They enjoyed the freedom to buy what they wanted and could afford. There were no shortages of basic goods, even during the Great Depression. Life was simple, sweet, and good.

Calle Fomento was a community where strong friendships took root. My aunts had friends on the street, and they would go to La Loma de la Cruz (the Hill of the Cross) for a view of the city and to do all of the things young people do. One of our neighbors, Caridad, became my grandmother's unconditional friend for life. My grandfather also became close friends with a man named Generoso, and with two other neighbors named Nené and Luis. After dinner when the sun went down, they would get together to talk politics and play dominoes in the clammy tropical evening.

Imagine a Cuba before 1959 when neighbors and citizens could sit down outside and openly discuss politics without persecution, without fear of being reported on, without fear of incarceration or death. In that long-gone Cuba, my family and their friends had freedom of speech. Freedom existed in Cuba from the birth of the republic through Batista's dictatorship. Fidel universally stamped out these basic rights and obliterated all traces of liberty from Cuba.

A Family Tragedy

Cuba was keeping up with technology, and there was a school on almost every city corner. Men and women became pharmacists, physicians, engineers, entrepreneurs, and so on. In addition to excellent, free public education to the eighth grade, there were private schools all over every city. There were also trade schools. For example, if you wanted to become a mechanic, baker, chef, hair stylist, florist, electrician, refrigeration technician, mason, plumber, or secretary, you would enroll in a trade school. There were even schools to become a housewife. All of these trades fueled private enterprise, which in turn fueled Cubans' desire to become successful and to fulfill their dreams. In Holguín, my oldest uncle, Valito, was no exception, and he enrolled in business courses to advance himself.

Then in 1933, the unimaginable happened. Valito committed suicide.

Ever since I can remember, my uncle Valito's tragic, self-inflicted death has been a mystery. From the little information I have been able to garner, I came to understand that, while at a family gathering, he committed a youthful indiscretion that today would be considered harmless. I seem to remember my mother telling me he had had too much to drink. However, in the early 1930s, youthful foolishness was a very big deal. A relative told my grandfather, and my grandfather reprimanded my uncle. My uncle was sensitive and prone to depression, so he was thrown into a state of inner anguish and despair.

Valito started talking to friends and neighbors about suicide, but no one told my grandparents, who would have lovingly told him that his indiscretion was forgiven and forgotten. They did not know about his growing despair, though, and soon Valito became so depressed that he shot himself right in my grandparents' backyard. The young do not realize that death is forever. The young do not realize the pain, sorrow, misery, and despair they will leave behind. How could these people who could have avoided such a tragedy live with themselves? Many of them came to Valito's wake and funeral. That's people for you.

Tragedy affects people in different ways, but usually grieving brings acceptance and healing. My grandparents, my mother, my aunts, and my uncle grieved deeply. Imagine how horrible and painful it was for my grandfather to lose his brightest son in such a senseless, tragic way. How his heart must have ached. Yet he made it through this profound loss. Perhaps he realized that he had to go on for the sake of his other children.

For my grandmother, it was different. Valito's death was the beginning of madness for her. The day my grandmother buried her son was the day that the light went out for her. She was traumatized for life. Her son's suicide seemed to confirm to her that she was destined to live a sad, miserable life.

Everyone tried to help her, but to no avail. My grandmother closed all of the front windows and the front door. She shut the whole world out, not realizing in her pain that she had two daughters who would be dating soon. The madness continued, with depression and withdrawal taking over. She did not bathe or comb her hair. She never drank water and would seldom eat. She wanted to die to be with her son.

Who am I to judge a mother grieving the tragic death of a child? Yet I can't help but think that, after a period of profound grieving, my grandmother needed to get up, look at her other children, and thank God for their lives.

She was unable to do this without professional help. She needed to go to Mazorra, the psychiatric sanatorium outside

Havana, which was known for good care. However, there was a stigma attached to psychiatric illnesses at the time, so she did not go. Instead, she sank deeper and deeper into depression and wallowed in her madness and lack of self-care. My grandfather stopped building houses.

Not long after Valito's death, my mother started school. Perhaps because my mother was the youngest and life at home was so imbued with sadness and tragedy, her father and aunts enrolled her in a special school, the Colegio Montesinos, which was a private Montessori grammar school that ran through the equivalent of junior high school. My mother was smart and loved school, so she excelled there.

In her childhood pictures, my mother has the saddest expression. She adored her mother, despite her illness. In her devotion, she became the hero child. She would come home from school and force her mother to bathe. While she tried to untangle her mother's hair, her mother fought her and hurled all kinds of insults. Yet my mom persisted. She accepted the insults of this poor, grieving, mad soul with the loving tenderness and caring that only a child can give.

Finally, someone convinced my grandmother to take up knitting. This was therapeutic for her, but she never quite returned to a normal life. Her front windows and door remained closed most of her life. She never went to the store, to a birthday party, or to visit a neighbor.

By this time, the best young years of her two oldest daughters were almost gone. They stopped going to parties and dances, and although they were beautiful, no one wanted to go to the house of a madwoman to court her daughters. These two aunts never married, and family of origin ties became stronger. The bonds that formed sustained them. After Fidel betrayed Cuba, traumatized Cuban society, and crafted a national tragedy that brought more pain and more loss, they leaned on one another more than ever. That was the silver lining in an extremely dark cloud.

Despite the impact of her mental illness on the family, my grandmother's surviving children and my grandfather did not resent her. I truly believe that their hearts were filled with compassion for her. I never witnessed or heard any hard feelings expressed. They loved her, respected her, and took care of her. As a child, I could see something was not right, but this was my family. They loved me and I loved them, unconditionally. I cherish the memories of my time with my grandmother and my aunts. In spite of it being a somber home, I remember with fondness the many times I sat in my grandmother's dining room, she in one rocking chair and I in the other.

Cuba kept progressing. There was no stopping it. There was still poverty, but there was also a strong middle class, most of whom had once been poor and had bettered their lot through hard work and frugality.

Batista continued to be a sinister—some say evil—power behind the scenes of Cuban government. His control of the military ensured that presidents served at his will. Yet despite the turbulent political situation, daily life and business for most Cubans was uninterrupted. Cuba was recovering from the crash. Cuba was still the number one sugar producer and exporter in the world, and by 1937 sugar was back to selling for $1.76 a pound.[7]

Four

The Golden Years

No one imagined that when President Prío was elected in 1948, he would be the last constitutionally elected president of the country. No one imagined that in four years a Batista coup would bring the opportunity the communists were waiting for, and that Cubans had only eleven years of freedom left.

President Prío had made it very difficult for the communist party to function, but he was not able to outlaw it totally. The Cuban Communist Party used the common communist tactic of going underground by joining the Orthodox Party (a faction of the *Auténtico* Party). Not everyone in the Orthodox Party (a.k.a. the People's Party) was a communist, yet all of the high-ranking communists were members of this left-leaning party. It was made up of liberals and radicals: the 1917 Marxist crowd, the social justice crowd, the utopians, the socialists, the progressives, and the agrarian- reformists. Although all of these factions had different goals and plans, they were branches of the same tree. Eventually, communism would subsume them all, as it always does with such coalitions.

When my parents got married, they ate their dinner sitting on wooden cartons. They saved up for a brighter future.

"When your father brought his salary home from the bakery, I made sure to save, if only a few cents," my mother told me. "If I had three pennies, I would save one and spend two," she told me many years later. Savings were the way to make dreams come true in those simpler, happier days.

While my parents were building a life for themselves, Cuba was enjoying a prosperous post–World War II economy. Private enterprise and a capitalist economy were continuing to improve Cubans' standard of living. Many refer to the forties as Cuba's golden years. By 1949, sugar was king again.

A small sugar tax provided funds dedicated to education. Public grammar and high schools were built in every city, and they were staffed with college-educated teachers. Public schools were added in *el campo* as well, staffed by teachers who, after graduating from college, were required to commit to work in a country school for one full year. Cuba's investment in education raised her to third among Latin American countries in education and literacy.[8]

Some among the poor were climbing up the financial ladder and becoming comfortable middle-class men and women. Those willing to work hard, like my father, got ahead. My father recognized that there was no shame in honest work, no matter how humble. He started out working at age twelve in any job he could find. He moved produce crates and did other manual labor. His big, developed hands revealed many years of hard, physical work, and one of his fingernails was deformed as the result of catching it in a crate. Laziness was not in his vocabulary.

Cubans were wealthy in spirit. They didn't put anyone down because they were poor or had less or because they lived in a humble neighborhood. That is really an American thing. Cuban people respected one another. I went to modern homes like those in El Reparto Peralta, a well-to-do suburb in Holguín. I admired the homes, and I remember being inspired. I also went to many a humble home with my parents, and not once did I hear my parents make any derogatory comments.

With all its socioeconomic levels, the republic was robust. Cuba was an up-and-coming and happy place. Until I was about age seven or so, I remember that Cubans always had smiles on their faces. Before Fidel's persecution and before the progressive dismantlement of Cuba, most Cubans looked on the bright side, toward the light of a better tomorrow.

Soon my mother became pregnant. She immediately began thinking of baby names.

"There was a pile of crumpled, discarded papers on the floor with rejected names on them," I remember her telling me. "I would stop for a while and do my chores and come back to the table to write down more names."

She was a young bride in love and full of love for the child she carried. For a girl, she finally decided on a combination of my father's and her names, taking the "o" off Mario and adding Blanca to christen my sister Mariblanca.

A black midwife delivered my sister at home. This was standard practice in 1949. If the baby was breech, the mother was immediately taken to a hospital. Just a few years later, by the mid-1950s, most babies in the cities were delivered in the cities' main hospitals or in maternity *clinicas*, which were private hospitals.

My father worked hard every day. He had only a grammar school education, but he had initiative and a strong work ethic. After he and my mother had been married for a while, he left the bakery and began to sell goods, such as cologne, talcum powder, and beauty products, door to door, first on a bicycle and then on a motorcycle. He was good with numbers and had a good business mind. He also had mottos—the customer was always right and the early bird got the worm—so he got up before everyone else and got to the customers first.

Little by little, they saved to buy more basic needs. Sturdy, plain wood, mission-style furniture was purchased that they expected to use for a lifetime. They worked hard so they could have a set of Sunday-best clothes. Years later in the United States, Fidel's supporters and the social justice crowd would scornfully call people like us rich. How mistaken they were!

Batista was running for president again and was elected Cuba's president from 1940–1944. Batista was part black, part Indian, and part white. (His election illustrates that Cuba before Fidel was a racially integrated society, including in the highest positions of power.) Prior to his election in 1940, Batista recognized the underground communist party, *Partido Unión Revolucionaria*, as a legal political party and did not impose restrictions on communist propaganda. Batista's actions facilitated communist infiltration of Cuba and its ultimate takeover, albeit he did not intend these results at all.

There was a sinister foreign presence in Cuba during the 1940s too: the United Soviet Union wanted a presence in the Caribbean to vex the United States and bring communism to Latin America.

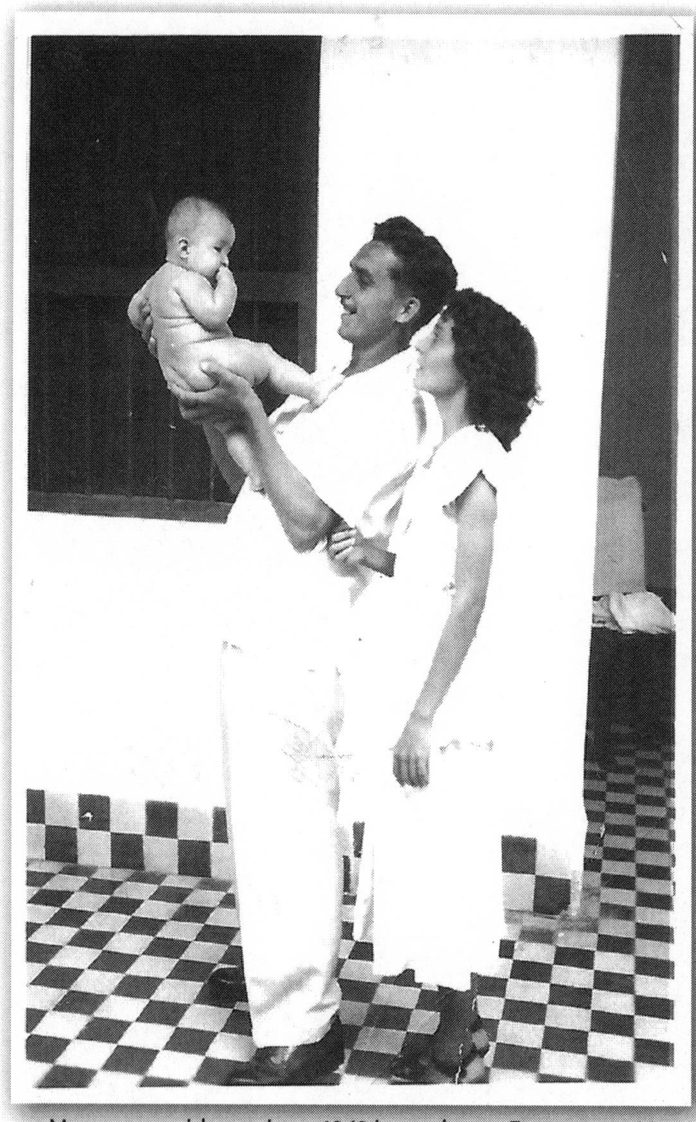

My parents with my sister, 1949 in our house Fomento #144

1950s

Five

Batista's Coup

When President Prío's term was about to end, the Orthodox Party had a good chance of winning the next election. Batista recognized that possibility. On March 10, 1952, just before the elections, he overthrew Prío's government in a military coup with minimal bloodshed.

Some suggest that the United States supported Batista's coup because of their concerns about communism.[9] The fact that the American ambassador recognized the new government before month's end makes this theory very likely.

The Cuban people chafed under Batista's imposed regime, and resistance rose. It seemed that everyone resented Batista and his coup. Good people with no agenda other than to return Cuba to legal elections were involved in the resistance, which was also supported by university students, academia, and various political parties and factions. All major newspapers in Cuba called for immediate elections. Cubans were fuming.

Batista responded by temporarily suspending the constitution, canceling elections, and declaring himself prime minister. He immediately appointed to high cabinet positions some of the thugs who had helped him with the coup. Batista never called it a coup; he took credit for a "no-bloodshed change of government," as if his interfering with elections were a desirable thing.

Batista made it clear that anyone found conspiring against his government would be dealt with severely. It was rumored that anyone who was a threat to Batista's power or who seriously opposed his government would be visited by two of his henchmen who would make the person drink a quart of castor oil. A quart! As a result, some people died, and some people had intestinal problems for the rest of their lives. Others were tortured in other ways. Some fled Cuba in fear. Batista continued to go after the top people of the political opposition, but he still did not interfere with ordinary people's liberties, nor did he stand in the way of Cuba's progress. Unions were strong. Roads were built and repaired, drains and aqueducts improved, and good-quality buildings constructed. Many big construction projects were awarded to Cuban unions, some of whose members and many of whose leaders were communists. Productivity increased.

Despite this barbarism, Batista never went after ordinary, everyday people. This does not make what he did right, but it does illustrate that the application of Batista's brutality was narrower in scope than Fidel's would be. Cuban cities, beaches, and the countryside were all open for use, and domestic and international travel between Cuba and the United States was unrestricted. Cuba still belonged to Cubans. Batista was far from harmless, but time would prove that his evil was not enough to destroy Cuba. Fidel's was. Many years later, Batista would seem almost benign when compared to the communist dictator who followed him.

This was illustrated to me in the summer of 1973. Our family was visiting my mother's cousin in New York City when we heard the news that Batista had died. The silence from my parents, my mom's cousin, and his wife was deafening.

"Batista is dead," my mother said calmly.

"Yes," responded her cousin.

To me it seemed that so much was said in those few words. They never liked Batista and wanted him ousted, and yet there wasn't an ounce of hatred toward him or any sense of jubilation that he was dead. Perhaps, along the way, Cubans who disliked Batista and wanted him out realized they might have overreacted. Perhaps they forgave Batista unconsciously, when his tyranny paled in the face of Fidel's. I don't know. I did not dare to ask.

My mother with my sister 1950 in the back of our house, aljíbe on left, zaguán back left, water filter next to back window, three windows on left one of my grandfather's rental

Six

ENTER FIDEL

Before the coup, a young man ran for a cabinet position in the Orthodox Party, and some say he was sure to win. Batista's coup thwarted that. This young man was Fidel Alejandro Castro Ruz.

In just a few years, it would become evident that the Castro brothers—Fidel and his little brother, Raúl—would stop at nothing to have permanent total power in Cuba. Time would show that the Soviet Union, through the two Castro brothers, would realize its goal and find firm footing in the Western world. It now had a base of operations just ninety miles from the United States from which to export communism and discord to the rest of Latin America. History shows that only a small percentage of Cubans against Batista were communists, but with Fidel's help, Cuban communists were able to infiltrate, take over, and totally steal the revolution, burying its original republican goals.

Who was this young man who captured the imagination of a country and then led it down a rabbit hole?

Who was this man who in just a few years would strip my parents of everything they worked and sacrificed for? Our humble family business, gone. Our car, gone. Our modest trips to the beach, gone. Who was this man who would leave me shoeless and with ill-fitting clothes and would make me climb the rail-less, steep stairs to the bell tower to prepare for my first communion in hiding? Who was this man who would make us write the communist year slogan on top of our notebook every day? Who was this man who would make it a crime to throw a paper airplane out the window? Why would my father be thrown in prison on trumped up charges? Who could be so cruel as to take Christmas and *el Día de los Reyes* and so many other simple pleasures away from children?

Who was the man whose betrayal would take hold of my mother's brain and eat at it for the next three decades until the only thing she could remember was, *Mi Cubita, mi Cubita*, how I loved you and how I lost you."

* * *

At the University of Havana, other students referred to Fidel as *el loco*, the crazy one, who carried a gun.[10] Those who remember Fidel, as does an acquaintance of mine who attended the university at the same time, remember him as always being at the center of one radical group or another. His alliance with the various groups or gangs shifted, depending on which side was convenient for him at the time.

Most students laughed at the radical crazies, and Fidel never forgot anyone who laughed at him, challenged him, or even just disagreed with him. He was vindictive, never forgetting the name or the face of someone who crossed him, whether in fact or in his mind.[11] He was obsessed with political meetings and, if he could get there, was at the center of any political turmoil in Latin America.

Fidel was and is an egomaniac and a fanatic, and egomaniacs and fanatics need someone to hate. In Fidel's case, it was the United States. It is clear that Fidel's hatred for the United States was deeply rooted in him from an early age, because by the time he was at the university, he never missed an opportunity to let it show. His hatred was fueled further by some fellow students and faculty who were also anti-American. When Fidel came into power, many of his political decisions were driven by that hatred.

Despite all of the bravado, Fidel was also driven by an inferiority complex. He wanted to be somebody. His heroes were Hitler and Mussolini. In his university years, he was often seen in front of mirrors imitating Adolph Hitler's tirade/speech gestures.[12] On the flip side of his sense of inferiority, Fidel suffered from grandiosity and had a reputation for thinking he knew everything about everything. Time would show that Fidel's egotism would be one element that contributed to the ruin of Cuba. In truth, there were really only two things Fidel was very good at: sports and deceit. Yet fortune often favored Fidel. Luck seemed to be on his side to an inordinate degree.

Soon after Batista's coup, Fidel gathered a group of friends. They armed themselves to attack Batista's army at Cuartel Moncada, the country's main residence for the military. Fidel told the men and women who joined him that he selected Moncada with the objective of obtaining arms for the cause. However, through the Moncada attack, Fidel really sought to make a great impact on *el pueblo*, the common people. He thought that the people of Santiago would join in the attack and make themselves the center of opposition.

Just as Hitler used the crisis and chaos of the Weimar Republic in pre–Nazi Germany to seize the opportunity to become known, Fidel used the Cuban people's anger at Batista and his coup to gain renown. Just as Hitler, with his failed Beer Hall Putsch coup, attempted to secure momentum for his Nazi movement, so too Fidel, by attacking the Moncada, sought to create momentum for his cause.

Fidel selected July 26, 1953, to assault Moncada because July 25 was the feast of Santiago's patron saint. It was carnival time in a city that produced the world's best rum. With rum selling for a nickel, Fidel thought everyone would be drunk, including the army. Well, everyone was drunk all right, except the army. This was Batista's army and, although Batista came from *el pueblo*, he was an educated military man. His army was always ready. It responded to the unprovoked attack like any military would. Fidel's campaign turned out to be a bloody fiasco that created chaos and panic in the city. On top of that, the people of Santiago failed to join the movement. Many of Fidel's men were killed. Fidel ran away to the Siboney region and his brother ran in another direction.

There are some who say Fidel did not even take part in the actual attack but orchestrated it from a distance. I don't find this hard to believe. Fidel was no George Washington, who on more than one occasion rode at the very front of the battle. Fidel was no José Martí, who rode in front of his men, leading the way on a white horse. Those who fought in La Sierra with Fidel remember his having a hole digger with him at all times to dig tunnellike holes large enough for him to crawl into because he was terrified of Batista's air force.[13]

In spite of poor planning and the catastrophic, bloody results of the attack, there is no doubt that Moncada was the beginning of Fidel Castro's history. The government's horrendous brutality toward the movement members who were arrested right after the attack is well known. It is very probable that this was what Fidel really wanted, because it tipped public sentiment toward him and his followers. Some Cubans, including my parents, thought the attack was a stupid maneuver, but to most, Fidel's decision to stand up to the state against great odds seemed valorous. The populace was swept up by the man; they thought he would lead them to their goal of a democratic constitutional republic. They were angry and despised Batista. They had no way of knowing that Fidel was manipulating them and would betray them and their cause.

Fidel filled a vacuum. He gave the revolution a face and a name to rally around. Moncada was the beginning of Cuba's love affair with Fidel; a love affair that lasted until 1961.

How they loved you, Fidel. How they loved you!

A while after Moncada, the Archbishop of Santiago, Monsignor Pérez Serantes, interceded for Fidel by working out a deal with the military. If Fidel turned himself in, he would not be executed. Raúl was part of the deal and also turned himself in. An evil man can be a lucky man. The monsignor's intervention saved Fidel and Raúl's lives.

How different, I wonder, would Cuba's future have been had the monsignor not interfered? Yet how could he have known that Fidel would persecute and kill Catholics? How could he have known that Fidel would keep churches open in name only? At the time he only wanted to stanch Cuba's bleeding.

I remember many years later in the 1960s; Monsignor Serantes visited our parish in Holguín. He was quite advanced in age at the time. When the monsignor died, it was rumored that Fidel went to his funeral, in spite of the persecution of the Catholic Church that he had perpetrated.

Fidel was tried for insurrection and found guilty. One judge abstained, stating that sedition was justified when it opposed an illegal government. Batista immediately fired the abstaining judge. His name was Manuel Urrutia Lleó. Later, in 1959, he would become the first figurehead president appointed by Fidel.

Fidel was sentenced to fifteen years in prison. But before sentencing, he was allowed to speak to the court. He stated, "History will absolve me."[14] After Fidel went to prison, his "history will absolve me" speech—largely a treatise on the ends justifying the means and an attempt to cast himself as a martyr—was reconstructed, printed, and circulated underground, making Fidel a household name in Cuba.

Few Cubans knew that Fidel had borrowed the arrogant phrase from Hitler.

Batista woke up to the dangers of communism and decided to outlaw the communist party. Batista intuitively knew the Moncada attack was much more than retaliation for his coup. After all, who in his right mind would attack Cuartel Moncada? Only someone who was insane or who had an agenda—or both. It was clear that Batista soon realized that there was something different about Fidel, that Fidel was a radical of the worst kind. But it was too late; Fidel's propaganda was spreading like wildfire.

As Fidel went to jail to serve his sentence, his group became known as Movimiento 26 de Julio,* the M-26-7. The colors of the movement were red, white and black, and they appeared on hats and movement propaganda. Many in the Orthodox group were impressed by the attack on the Moncada fortress. They and various socialist and student groups saw that indeed the gate to revolution had opened, so they worked to keep the movement alive while Fidel was in jail.

* * *

Cubans continued to strongly dislike Batista, but the economy was strong and there was free enterprise. Regardless of who was in power, the Cuban republic had a vibrant economy, religious freedom, and an excellent health-care system. There was freedom of movement, including the right to travel abroad.

---

* July 26 Movement.

As the movement against him grew, Batista called for elections. All opposition parties withheld candidates in protest because they thought the election was a sham. Consequently, Batista was elected to a four-year term. Although they voted in the elections, many Cubans did not recognize the elections as valid nor Batista as president. Cubans continued to resent the coup and the circumstances of Batista's subsequent election.

Perhaps things would have been different if the various political parties had entered candidates to oppose Batista, or if the Cuban people had forgiven Batista or had simply waited four years for the next elections. I wonder how many Cubans look back and ask themselves these same burning questions, the answers to which might have changed the fate of a nation.

After all, Batista's power was temporary; Fidel Castro has been in power for more than half a century.

But then, hindsight is twenty-twenty.

* * *

On May 16, 1955, Batista made another grave miscalculation—a disastrous mistake for him, and for Cuba. He declared amnesty for almost all prisoners. This included Fidel, his brother, Raúl; and approximately eighteen others who had participated in the Moncada attack. They were amnestied and their records were expunged.

After serving twenty months of a fifteen-year sentence, Fidel was free. He left Cuba and went to Mexico, which was still bleeding from the Cristiada Civil War. Atheist Marxist President

Plutarco Elias Calles was spearheading the curtailment of religious freedom, the expropriation of Catholic churches and schools, and the government assassination of hundreds of priests and nuns in Mexico.

If Fidel did not already have a plan to persecute and eradicate Christianity in Cuba and to turn Cuba into an atheist state, he certainly got a few clues as to how to go about it while in Mexico. In this environment, Fidel had no problem finding and joining underground leftist groups.

The Hardware Store on Fomento

During these years of factional political strife, my father was continuing to work hard on Calle Fomento. My parents opened a family business located in the living room and dining room of our home. The rest of the house was spacious, so this business move could be accommodated.

My father gave his simple business a simple name, La Quincalla (The Hardware Store). Juan, a carpenter who lived around the corner from my grandmother, built the shelves and counters. My father sold hardware, housewares, and personal goods. Sometimes his inventory depended on what the traveling salesmen were selling. My father stood by his motto that the customer was always right. If someone brought a purchase back with a concern, the item was replaced and/or the price refunded. My father truly was a good businessman, and in the Cuba of that time, it was not hard to make something of yourself if you wanted to.

My parents were not rich, but they spent money on the family. My mother bought my sister the dolls and toys she herself never had. She tried hard to give my sister pretty things. She bought nice fabric and had pretty dresses made for her. (Off-the-rack clothing was not common and was costlier.)

My mother always regretted not having more pictures from her childhood, so every year on her birthday, my sister got a new dress, went to the hairdresser, and had her picture taken professionally at a local studio. Mom wanted her kids to have a lot of pictures of their youth. Little did she know that she was capturing a history and a quality of life that Fidel would obliterate. For mere pennies she could get a package of nice photographs, though by the mid-1960s, the availability of quality paper and color inks had dwindled. My mother continued the tradition of yearly portraits with me until 1968, when loss of quality in the photos and loss of hope in my mother ended it.

My mother enrolled my sister in Colegio Montesinos, the school she herself had attended. She also enrolled her in dance and piano lessons and begged my father to buy a piano, even a used one, so my sister could practice.

"Not now," he told her. "We have to save money for a rainy day."

Well, they should have purchased the piano because the man they adored, Fidel, would ruin the Cuban economy and the value of the peso, which was on a par with the U.S. dollar when he came into power. My parents' savings lost nearly all of its value. In addition, my parents could not foresee that they would apply to leave their homeland on the Freedom Flights, resulting in the little devalued money they had saved being frozen and then seized by the government. Even if they had been allowed to keep their savings, during our last years in Cuba there were almost no essential products to buy and certainly no luxuries like a piano.

Revolution Brewing

While my parents were building a life for their family in Holguín, Fidel met Ernesto Che Guevara. Although trained as a physician, he did not practice medicine. Che claimed to be a Marxist, yet he lived a bohemian life, traveling through Latin America on his motorcycle. He became a global folk hero in the United States and other countries, where he was thought to be a heroic freedom fighter. He was in fact a murderer of the Cuban people.

While in Mexico, Fidel announced that he was leaving the Orthodox Party,[15] one of many feints to obscure his communist beliefs. Thereafter, for several years, he would periodically deny being a communist.

He and Che *began* to organize a rebel group to return to Cuba from Mexico. Oriente, farthest east on the island, had been the heart of the Cuban War of Independence, and Fidel and Che's plan was to make the province the heart of the movement. Indeed, more and more men from Oriente joined the movement, traveling to Mexico to join up with Fidel. From Mexico, Fidel and Che built their brand: the bearded, savior-like image of the *guerilleros* was fostered to deceive our nation and the world.[16]

In Havana, and then in other major cities, resistance to Batista began to take the form of sabotage and terrorism. Individual activist cells, communists and others, used cocktail bombs to spread carnage in the streets of Cuba, injuring and killing innocent people. Many of the bombers and other saboteurs backed Fidel. Public places and public transportation were the main targets. In addition to the lives and property lost, businesses suffered because people were afraid to patronize sporting events, bars, and restaurants. In order to turn a whole country against Batista and motivate it to fight, especially in the urban areas, there had to be blood in the streets. When Batista's army retaliated, there was more bloodshed. Often the Cuban and U.S. media reported a one-sided story, blaming all of the violence on Batista and ignoring the violence he was trying to stop.

The following December, Fidel; Che; Fidel's brother, Raúl; and good-hearted Camilo Cienfuegos, along with approximately eighty-one rebels, left Mexico and landed on Playa de los Colorados, a swampy area in Oriente. Under attack from the air force, some rebels were killed. Fidel, his brother, Che, and Cienfuegos headed for La Sierra Maestra, a mountain range in southeast Cuba.

Seven

La Sierra

La Sierra Maestra was the romantic, bohemian aspect of the revolution, which made Fidel a legend in the eyes of the Cuban people. They perceived him as fighting hard for them in all kinds of uncomfortable conditions: living with lice in rain and mud and enduring the air force air assaults. People saw Fidel as their savior, their *guerrillero*, their freedom fighter.

The *campesinos* of La Sierra, who were mostly small coffee growers, were good to Fidel. He could walk into any house, be well received, and set up headquarters. They welcomed him with open arms. Without their protection, Fidel would not have survived. Any one of them could have handed him over to the military. No one did.

Fidel had charisma. He was handsome and educated, and people were drawn to him. He had a college degree and was a lawyer. Of course, these trappings did not mean he had any class or dignity. Far from it.

There were many ways in which Fidel was not all that Cubans thought. Many of the farmers, who were ordinary people, owned the land they lived on. They loved and respected the land and its creatures. They only killed animals for food. Fidel's cruelty toward farm animals did not go unnoticed by the farmers. They showed distress and even hatred for Fidel when he attached explosives to pigs and chickens and blew them up right in front of them.[17]

However, despite their disgust at his actions, most *campesinos* were pro Fidel. Many farmers lost their homes and were displaced as a result of air strikes aiming for Fidel. Consequently, they resented the government. This did not make them communists, but in the early days of the revolution, it put them in Fidel's camp. They could not know that Fidel would strip them of their land and, in less than three years, thousands of farmers would die trying to save their farms from his imposed agrarian law or would be forcibly relocated to other provinces when they refused to give up their farms.[18]

Fidel was the most unfaithful person to a loving God and to a loving Cuban people. He betrayed everyone, even those who were good to him. Sometimes you read here and there, "Fidel is a good man; I can see it in his eyes." Fidel's eyes have never had any life in them; they have always been dead. I know it's very hard for some to believe that there are people who are just plain evil, but it's true, and Fidel Castro is one of them. When a sociopath gains power over a nation and a people, the results are horrendous. Combined with an antihuman political philosophy, like communism, nations are devastated. Cuba was no exception.

Fidel's group of rebels attracted people from all walks of life. Physicians, lawyers, engineers, architects, writers, newspaper reporters, artists, pharmacists, teachers, college professors, landowners, businessmen, *campesinos*, and ordinary city folk supported the revolutionary goals. Black, white, Asian, Indian, the wealthiest, the poorest, the most educated, and the least educated joined the cause. This revolution was never a social class revolution as Fidel has made the world believe. This revolution was a whole country, *todo un pueblo*, against Batista. For most, it was also a revolution to stop corruption and coups in Cuba. As a people, we wanted freedom, justice, and representative government. That was all. This normal human yearning was co-opted by Fidel and his minions and trampled down under the heavy boots of totalitarianism.

Other groups aligned themselves with the revolutionary forces in hopes of entering the expected new government. In the end, only one group prevailed—Fidel's—and, in actuality, not even the movement survived. Only the Castro brothers prevailed.

Bloody terrorist sabotage continued in the cities, especially in Havana and Santiago de Cuba. All of it was characterized as *La Revolución*. Fidel had a lot of protection in the hills, and he offered that protection to those who were running away from Batista. If you had been identified as part of the movement, saboteurs included, you were not safe in the city, so you ran to join Fidel. The movement turned into a revolution and the revolution turned into civil war.

The revolution was in full swing. Sometimes in history everything seems to come together just right. Every Cuban felt that way during the revolution to oust Batista. Every Cuban felt they were part of something big. My parents, along with most Cubans, disliked Batista with a passion, and they fully supported the revolution and Fidel. Later they would find out what strong dislike really was. But then, like most Cubans, my parents had Fidel Fever.

Eight

Child of the Revolution

I was born on February 20, 1958, in Holguín, Oriente, in a private maternity hospital. My mother told me later that I was in so much of a hurry to come into the world that she almost didn't make it to the clinic. I was a child of the revolution, and my parents strongly considered naming me Fidelia.

My early years were comfortable ones. My parents' business was doing well, thanks to their hard work, and initially they were able to give me all of the things that they had given my sister. We were not rich, nor were any of our neighbors, but my parents, like other Cubans on our street, were dedicated to providing for their families.

Fidel and Camilo were now household names, and the masses adored them. It was an exciting time to have a child in Cuba; a time when neighbors were able to meet outdoors to get the latest news from La Sierra. Victory was near; they could feel it in their bones! They would oust Batista and free elections would be held, they thought. No more coups, only constitutional elections.

I was too young to experience the euphoria and excitement of the revolution, but I heard about it later from my family. Fidel was their hero. Fidel was their savior. Cubans were delirious with Fidel. They were no longer infatuated with Fidel; they *loved* him. Their sincere love for him and faith in him made his subsequent betrayal of them even more painful.

Triumph and Promises

Batista knew the whole country hated him, and when the rebels entered and occupied Santiago for two days without any resistance from local police or the army, he finally realized even those closest to him had deserted him. The vice president was nowhere to be found. Batista recognized that he had no recourse and resigned his presidency, appointing an interim government to be headed by Colonel Cantillo and Carlos Manuel Piedra, the oldest Supreme Court magistrate. The provisional government was intended to keep order and to ready the way for free elections, which was one of the express goals of the revolution. Batista then invited a group of close friends for a New Year's Eve toast at his house near the military airport. He warned them of potential danger and advised them to be ready to leave. Then, around midnight on December 31, 1958, Fulgencio Batista left Cuba.[19]

* * *

It was New Year's Day 1959, and Batista was out. The whole nation had repudiated him. Yet Cubans soon would learn that, despite what Fidel said, Cuba's days of freedom, even in the form it took under Batista, had come to a close.

Fidel returned to Santiago and went directly to Cuartel Moncada to give his first post-Batista speech. The whole nation, filled with an incomparable joy, was glued to their radios and televisions. They loved Fidel. He was savior and redeemer, everyone's hero. Fidel took advantage of the country's jubilant mood and informally assumed the title of commander in chief of the military forces.

In his speech, Fidel brought up that it was in Santiago that the Americans had stolen the 1898 war from the Cuban people by not allowing the Cuban generals to take part in the truce talks. It was highly significant that Fidel made this anti-American statement in his very first victory speech, but Cubans, in their euphoria, didn't recognize it for the loaded statement it was. They didn't realize what a major role Fidel's anti-Americanism would play in their lives.

Fidel continued his speech, calling for the integration of rebel and military forces for the "good" of the country. He told the Cuban people that there would no longer be a dictator's state police. Instead, police would wear their uniforms with pride, ready to serve the people. He promised truce and fairness to men who had fought on both sides. He ended the eloquent speech with, "*Viva la Revolución!*"

Cubans poured out of their homes. They were elated and didn't hold back. There were thousands and thousands of men and women in Santiago's central park, where trees were decorated with holiday lights. It was pure joy, pure ecstasy.

Cubans had no idea what was coming. They had no idea how the man they adored would betray them, execute them, make them disappear, tear their families apart, starve them, and deprive them of basic goods and services. They had no idea of the misery their hero would impose on them over the next half century, or how he would destroy the republic on all levels. They had no idea how many *ahogados** and *desaparecidos*† would come! Thousands of talented Cubans would be thrown in jail to rot. Countless souls would needlessly die untimely deaths as a direct or indirect result of Fidel's actions, many of whose names only a loving God would know.

Before leaving Santiago, Fidel gave another electrifying speech. He promised to restore the capital of Cuba to Santiago, which was the capital in the 1500s before it was moved to Havana. Fidel stated that dictatorship had ended, and it would not be repeated. He promised one dictator would not replace another. He went on to praise the democratic electoral process and stated that the military would follow the rule of law established by the republic's constitution.

As soon as he finished his eloquent, misleading speech, Fidel sent a message to Colonel Cantillo stating he would not recognize the interim government, which Cantillo headed, and if Cantillo and Piedra didn't step down, they would have to

---

* Drowned [people].

† Missing [people].

answer to him.[20] Behind closed doors, Fidel's totalitarian regime had begun.

The March

Fidel's conquering march to Havana commenced. Every vehicle available joined the march with its lights on. My mom remembered the march as almost a religious procession. It moved very slowly from east to west. As Fidel, riding on a tank, made his way from Santiago to Havana, crowds of civilians from all walks of life joined the march and followed him. The solemn column grew by the thousands all along the way to Havana. It was an electrifying, emotional, and unifying march. As Fidel passed by each town or farm, he was hailed as a liberator and a hero.

Fidel entered Havana on January 8, 1959.

Havana residents greeted Fidel and the thousands who marched with him. Those who were there have never forgotten the indescribably joyous experience. Fidel took the stage and made another thrilling speech. He promised peace and harmony. Two doves landed on his shoulders. Luck was always on Fidel's side, even to the extent that two birds may have chosen his shoulders to roost. It could have been staged with bait and trained birds. Whether staged or a lucky coincidence, many saw this as a spiritual seal for Fidel's peace-and-harmony speech and his rule.

Deceit in Quick Stages

Looking back, Fidel's actions after his triumphant arrival in Havana clearly showed that he never meant to restore democratic elections to the republic and that he had totalitarian ideas from the beginning. However, the republic was in a daze and totally enamored of him. Fidel knew people would eventually realize what was happening, so he acted quickly to impose his totalitarian regime before large numbers of people woke up.

After entering Havana, Fidel played his first overt card. While Batista was retreating and setting up an interim government, Fidel had sent for Manuel Urrutia Lléo, the former judge who had abstained during his trial, and asked him to take over the presidency and to choose his own cabinet. Urrutia was an attorney and a man of character who enjoyed popularity with the Cuban people. He chose prime people, the cream of the crop, for the post-Batista cabinet.

Why would Fidel go to all this trouble? Why? Those who lived through the revolution kept asking this and they still wonder. Did Fidel enjoy the art of deception and chicanery that much that he would set up a dummy cabinet he had no intention of honoring?

* * *

Things seemed to be moving along smoothly toward governance by the constitution, but in May 1959 the Agrarian Reform Law was passed. Reportedly, this law was originally written in accordance with the revolution's goals to distribute *abandoned* government land to unlanded peasants. It did not provide for expropriation or redistribution of private property.

However, it was a slippery slope. Like most agrarian reforms, Cuba's agrarian law had its roots in the 1917 Russian Revolution; as such, it didn't take long for it to turn ugly. Soon reform turned into state-controlled socialization of agriculture, following the model of Stalin's 1929 forced collectivization. Fidel used agrarian reform to seize land either without compensation or for a meaningless token amount.

The real agenda behind Castro's agrarian reform was to establish "people's farms," which were nothing more than state enterprises like those of Stalin's Russia. Poor Cuban peasants who were not landowners were fooled. Rather than receiving a few acres of land, they were required to live on the people's farms, where they worked for a salary and had no rights of ownership or decision-making.[21]

A cascade of events started almost immediately. Fidel played the racism and illiteracy cards to manipulate world opinion—the opinion of a world that obviously didn't know Cuba's history when it came to race relations or education. Fidel announced the delay of general elections "until illiteracy is eliminated in Cuba,"[22] implying that Cuba's people of color and peasants needed education before they could be responsible voters.

Propaganda began to circulate that showed a *guajiro** holding a piece of chalk to a blackboard, learning to write. The world ate it up, but Fidel only fooled those who turned a blind eye to what was happening. People of all colors were integrated in Cuban society; there was no marginalized body of ignorant people, and illiteracy was already being minimized in

---

* A rustic.

55

Cuba by the huge expansion of schools under Batista. No one was on the fringes in Cuban society before Castro, including the independent, hardworking, smart, and self-sustaining peasants.

It is true that there were illiterate people in Cuba, and it is also true that there was more illiteracy in small towns and villages than in the city (this is true of almost all developing countries). Challenges for rural education included rural customs, availability of teachers, and the demands of the rural economy. While many farmers valued education for their children, it is also true that some farmers did not see the need for their children to go to school. Sometimes there was a lack of rural teachers because some returned to the city after serving their one-year rural commitment. It was a free country; no one put a gun to a teacher's head and forced him or her to stay in an unwanted job, and young professionals usually wanted to live in cities. Schooling was inconsistent but present in the country. My maternal grandparents and maternal aunts and uncles had this inconsistent schooling when they lived in the country.

Yet despite the challenges to rural education, in 1958 the Republic of Cuba was a predominantly literate nation. According to the archives of Cuba's Ministry of Education, in 1958 Cuba had an 82 percent literacy rate with 25,000 teachers in public schools, 1,206 of whom taught in rural schools. An additional 3,500 teachers provided education in private schools.[23]

Fidel cynically exploited the normal rural–urban gap in education to mislead and manipulate—and to postpone elections.

* * *

To support his divisive agenda within Cuba, Fidel had to suppress Cuba's true racial history. Fidel used all organs of propaganda to make the world believe that before the revolution, all Cuban blacks were unaccomplished and disenfranchised and that the revolution brought a new social order. Out came the propagandistic photo of a black child sitting with white children outside a school, and the world believed this was something new.

In reality, Cuba was an almost entirely integrated society, and black Cubans were the most educated and successful blacks in the region. Slave owners had been encouraged to educate slaves, and when slaves were freed in Cuba, they had no problem assimilating and becoming part of society. What raised people up in Cuba was not race, but education.

Before Fidel, black Haitians and Jamaicans immigrated to Cuba looking for a better life. Ironically, some of the black Jamaicans and Haitians who came to Cuba to support Fidel during the revolution ended up in jail as political prisoners when they too spoke up against Fidel's dictatorship.

Whether former slaves or black immigrants, some became more successful than others, the same as with whites and other ethnic groups. There were many university-educated blacks and many blacks in the police force and army, including national hero General Maceo. Were there poor blacks in Cuba before Fidel? Yes, but there were also poor whites. Was there room for improvement? Yes, there was, for all races.

Before Fidel, Cubans were very open about race and spoke about it with one another. In Cuba, ethnic words such as *negro,* *negra*[*], *chino, china,*[†] *blanco,* and *blanca*[‡] were said in affectionate description and were heard in the lyrics of many Cuban songs.

Mixed marriages were *not* illegal in Cuba, as they were in other parts of the world. Many preferred to marry within their own race, while others found the right partner in a different race.

Anything public—from education, to hospitals, to transportation, to pharmacies, to grocery stores—were open and available to all Cubans, regardless of race. As far back as 1908, a black Cuban who was head of the Senate, Martín Morúa Delgado, became alarmed when the private Independent Association for Blacks in Cuba, which was open only to blacks and of which he was a member, became large enough to organize its own political candidates based on race. He felt the idea was racist in nature, would do much harm to Cuba, and would undermine Cuba's integrated, racially harmonious society. Consequently, he introduced a law in the Senate, which passed, making it illegal for any political party to be made up of only one race.[24] Senator Delgado, himself black and one of the most patriotic and educated figures of his time, made it clear that Cubans were Cubans.

From the indigenous people to colonization, to slavery to the freeing of slaves, to the inclusion of blacks into society, to the immigration of Asians and to independence from

---

[*] Black man, black woman.

[†] Chinese man, Chinese woman

[‡] White man, white woman.

Spain—all of it—had been taught in Cuban schools until 1961. After that, Cuba's true history, including the true history of its race relations, was suppressed by Fidel's regime.

* * *

Not surprisingly, the government officials that Fidel set up didn't last long. The new prime minister began to bump heads with Fidel and resigned. Fidel appointed himself prime minister and added one condition—he and only he would be president of the cabinet, a role usually held by the president of the country. Thus, President Urrutia's headaches began.

As soon as he became prime minister, Fidel announced yet another postponement of general elections. This was another obvious sign that this traitor, who was one of our own, had no intention of restoring the republic. Cuba already had a great economy, a three-branch form of government, and a people who loved their country and were committed to voluntary works of charity and education. Fidel could have built on this fine foundation to construct a fine and flourishing nation, the kind of nation Cubans dreamed of and were willing to work hard for. If Fidel had wanted to legitimately head the cabinet, all he had to do was run for president. Further, the whole country would have called for a constitutional convention to allow presidents to run for consecutive terms. Fidel would have accomplished what Machado wanted because the whole nation loved him. The Cuban people would have elected him over and over again.

Instead Fidel chose the iron hand.

The Executions Begin

Executions started in Cuba right after Fidel took over. Batista's regime was unjust and at times brutal to many who had joined the July 26 Movement. Consequently, as soon as Fidel took power, a vocal part of the population demanded justice for those who had previously abused power.

Not all of the military abused power; not all government employees abused power. Many military personnel and government officials and employees had silently backed Fidel and wanted to be part of the restored government. They never thought Fidel would execute them. Yet despite his promises of amnesty and harmony, he did just that.

Fidel assigned Che, a foreigner, to the post of head executioner at Fortaleza de La Cabaña (a fortress and prison in Havana) and left his brother, Raúl, in charge of trials and executions in Santiago. He tossed aside the 1940 constitution, which stated that the death penalty applied only to crimes involving the killing of military personnel. Fidel started adding other offenses that were punishable by death, such as being a supporter of the old regime, a war criminal, or an antirevolutionary. He did not define either "war criminal" or "antirevolutionary," and he kept adding new reasons to execute people as he pleased.

It became clear that Fidel would get rid of anyone who had been part of the Batista government at any level. Anyone who spoke against the injustice was thrown in prison or executed.

Some high-ranking Batista military, along with some not so high, were in jail awaiting trial. Many Cubans were still carried away by the euphoria of the revolutionary triumph and were acting from emotion and not from reason or ethics. They demanded *el paredón*[*] without realizing that without just trials and just sentences, some innocent people were being tortured and killed.

In Santiago, which had been the central base for Batista's military, Raúl allowed few trials, and those that were allowed were mock trials. Many people who should have received jail time were executed. Everything was carried out so fast. In the Fortaleza de La Cabaña in Havana, Che continued *el paredón*.

In Holguín, where I lived, executions were carried out right outside La Salida de San Andrés behind Loma del Fraile. The spot was designated to execute anyone associated with Batista's government, guilty or not. From their windows, nearby residents could see the new militia parade these poor souls to the lot to be executed. They saw friends, neighbors, and acquaintances being led away. From their houses they could hear the gunshots. Many Cubans had nervous breakdowns, losing their minds just watching what was happening to their loved ones, friends, and fellow Cubans. The revolution was not supposed to turn out this way. Already, so soon, it had blood on its hands. Already, so soon, it had committed so many unforgivable sins.

With Raúl and Che directing, Fidel was able to execute most of Batista's military and many government employees within a few days of entering Havana. In one day alone, there

---

[*] The firing squad ("the wall").

were approximately one hundred executions. News of the executions was broadcast on public television, and word quickly got around Cuba about a new and different abuse of power that was leading to another dictatorship and no justice. The hundreds of executions in Santiago, Havana, and other cities tarnished the revolution in the eyes of many in Cuba and abroad. But the memories of people who did not live through it are short.

If Fidel Did Not Like the Outcome of a Trial...

Forty-three army air force pilots who attacked La Sierra under military orders were tried. When the courts acquitted them because they were obeying orders, Fidel stated that he did not like the verdict. He had them tried again. He did not give up until they were found guilty—the antithesis of due process. After being tried a second time and found guilty, they were given thirty-year sentences. These pilots were very lucky that they were not executed, and some were paroled before completing their sentences.

The mechanics who serviced the air force planes were also tried and given lighter sentences.[25] The mechanics! I have to wonder whether Fidel's brutality was really personal revenge for the fear he experienced during the bombings from Batista's air force in La Sierra.

Fidel was carrying out his own mini–French Revolution. No one associated with the Batista regime in any shape or form was spared. Fidel was all about getting even; all about vengeance. In Fidel's own words, "Not even a puppet will remain here with the head on its shoulders; there will not be as much as a hitching post left standing; no one will be saved."[26]

When some top people in the revolution began to question where Fidel was taking Cuba, Fidel's words and actions made clear that he was rapidly taking liberties away from Cubans and moving Cuba both to the left and into a totalitarian state. This was totally contrary to the revolution's goal of returning Cuba to a lawful republic.

Those close to Fidel thought their proximity to him would make it easier for them to topple him, and they tried from the inside but did not succeed. One by one, Fidel found them out and got rid of them, either by execution or imprisonment. Some simply disappeared, never to be heard from again. Others were barely able to escape the country with their lives. Fidel even got rid of anyone whom he imagined to be a potential enemy. He had an advantage: he knew the men and women who had fought with him, and he knew the ideals they had fought for, so discerning dissent was easy for a person as canny and vigilant as he.

Also in early 1959, Fidel forced an action that was one of the first steps in the destruction of the Cuban economy. He called for a meeting with Felipe Pazos, economist and president of Cuba's National Bank, in which he told Mr. Pazos that the National Bank should facilitate the financing of agrarian reform with a sizeable low interest loan. Pazos declined, explaining Cuban banking law and why such an action would not be in the best financial interest of the country. In response, Fidel made it clear to this economist and banker that the bank would make the loan at the interest he indicated or else.[27] Fidel thought he was an expert in every field. In reality Fidel was good at two things: deceit and sports.

Visit to the United States

In April, Fidel visited the United States and met with Vice President Nixon. Some subscribe to the notion that President Eisenhower's decision not to meet with him was the reason that Fidel turned to the Soviet Union. This perception played perfectly into Fidel's hand, but it had no basis in fact. The United States had already recognized Cuba's new government. Additionally, Cuba did not need Soviet assistance. Cuba's economy had suffered somewhat in some main cities due to anti-Batista sabotage and the1959 post-revolutionary vandalism; however, 1957 had been Cuba's most prosperous economic year, with $680 million in sugar sales.[28] If Fidel had not collectivized the republic's businesses and industry, Cuba's vibrant economy would have prospered without outside subsidies. Further, Fidel had the opportunity to meet with some of the top economists in the United States and chose not to.[29] Instead, it was all about ego with Fidel. He had found his excuse to agitate against the United States, and he managed to convince the world that he had been slighted by the U.S. government.

Everyone Loves a Parade

As the months progressed, abuse of power surfaced everywhere in Cuba. On May 1, 1959, traditional May Day parades took place all over the island. The biggest parade was in Havana.

Since the inception of labor unions in Cuba, every elected president had attended the parade. As part of the May Day parade, it was a Cuban tradition for the union workers to present their demands publically, stating what rights they wanted Congress to grant.

Fidel calmly waited for the president of the national labor unions to present his demands. Evil can be so patient, so calm. Fidel was very calm. When the union demands were presented to him, instead of honoring the tradition of every president before him, Fidel had the president of the national union arrested and thrown in jail.

This was yet another sign to the Cuban people that they were living under a different kind of government. The constitution was no longer guiding the country. Something was very wrong. This was not freedom. The better informed or better educated public could no longer deny that the republic was turning into a totalitarian dictatorship. The cabinet went into crisis, some members agreeing with Fidel and some not.

Social Class Discord

Next, Fidel began to encourage discord among social classes, which was a signal that private property was in jeopardy. All over the island there were worker takeovers of privately owned companies, and many privately owned automobiles were confiscated from the families of men who had been top officials in Batista's regime.

The people Fidel originally placed in power, purportedly to restore the republic, became uneasy.

Fidel immediately announced that those who were not on the side of his government were antirevolutionary *gusanos.*[*] This type of vulgar, demeaning speech to the masses and the world would become more and more frequent in his public rants. Fidel knew the less-informed and less-educated masses were still enamored of him, saw him as the messiah who could do no wrong, and would turn against the accused.

As disastrous events accumulated, President Urrutia, realizing he was a puppet president, declared a state of emergency and announced that he wanted to restore elections immediately. Fidel objected. Urrutia made it clear to the cabinet that he did not like where Fidel was taking Cuba and fell into conflict with cabinet members, some of whom still supported Fidel.

Fidel wasted no time. He accused Urrutia of treason. Urrutia resigned and was lucky to escape Cuba alive.

More and more Cubans began to question agrarian "reform" and all of the other "reforms" Fidel was passing. Fidel knew the cat was out of the bag.

Knowing how the Cuban masses would respond, Fidel played his next brilliant and evil card.

"I cannot govern with this cabinet," Fidel told the masses. "I want to leave Cuba for the good of the people." Then he resigned as prime minister, stating that the cabinet's anticommunist views were making it impossible to govern Cuba. It was a masterstroke. Yes, even evil can be brilliant. He knew the masses would answer as they did.

"No, Fidel, you stay, you stay," the masses cried out.

---

[*] Maggots; worms.

"What should I do with the cabinet?" Fidel asked.

"*Paredón, paredón,*" answered the masses.

The masses asked for the cabinet to be put to death! They wanted Fidel. Yet, many in that crowd who shouted for Fidel ended up dying at the hands of his regime or having to flee Cuba. Of those who survived and remained on the island, nearly all were to suffer in the misery that was communist Cuba.

Fidel's propaganda worked, and the entire cabinet resigned. The star-studded cabinet, the cream-of-the-crop cabinet that was to restore the constitutional Republic of Cuba to the Cuban people, was gone. Fidel filled all key cabinet positions with members of the communist party. If Fidel did not intend to turn Cuba into a communist regime, he clearly understood that communism was a means to his goal: Fidel Castro as Cuba's lifetime dictator and utopian king.

From this point on Fidel really began to run rampant and trample everything that was good in Cuba.

Fidel began to dismantle the infrastructure of the Cuban economy. He replaced Felipe Pazos, head of the National Bank, with Che who knew absolutely nothing about economics or banking. The appointment was so strikingly erroneous that it was completely obvious to those paying attention that Fidel was taking Cuba from a traditional economy to a very dark place.

Not even the two men who rode with him into Havana got a pass. Fidel had Matos arrested after Matos questioned where Fidel was taking Cuba. He was tried in a circus trial, found guilty, and sentenced to twenty years in prison. Cienfuegos mysteriously disappeared, never to be seen or heard from again. So many heroes of the revolution were betrayed.

By now, more of the noncommunist intellectuals, other well-educated individuals, and some of the middle class had Fidel all figured out. In contrast, many of the poor and the misinformed, who are always easy prey for deceit, were still infatuated with their dictator. Reality had not trickled down the social classes quite yet. The masses were not aware that their country, their hopes, and their dreams were being stolen. The communist influence in Cuba was stronger. The original goals of the revolution were becoming more and more distant. Fidel had so many opportunities to do the right thing for Cuba. Fidel was given a torch, yet he extinguished it and chose darkness.

Despite all of the executions and imprisonments and the creeping communism, daily life had not changed for average Cubans like my family, who had not yet become targets. We still had food, our businesses, and our cars, making it easy for some to say that things weren't so bad. Hunger had not yet set in, so many in the middle class, the lower middle class, and the poor had not yet realized that they too would become Fidel's victims.

Many years later, my mother told me how everything started to become clearer to her after Camilo's disappearance. It was very difficult for her to admit that Fidel had deceived the Cuban people so thoroughly. Ordinary Cubans began to break through their denial and began to see Fidel for what he was.

Even so, my mother recalled that she was not totally disillusioned with Fidel. Though the fast-moving events had disturbed my mother, she still supported Fidel. He had that kind of power over people. Every woman in Cuba, I think, was taken with him. He was handsome and charismatic. Still in denial, my mom would go to her parents' house and argue with her family, who had already recognized Fidel's betrayal.

Camilo's disappearance right after Matos's arrest brought about the strongest indication of what was to come. Regular Cubans, like my parents, were jolted into recognizing that things were not as they thought. Fidel had managed to fool the Cuban citizenry long enough to steal Cuba, but he never fooled—and he knows it—any Cuban when it came to Camilo.

Strangely, as with others he betrayed, years later Fidel proclaimed Camilo a national hero. Perhaps he was acknowledging Camilo's contribution to his rise to power, or maybe it was part of his ruse. At any rate, on the anniversary of the announced date of Camilo's disappearance, all students were pulled out of school to spread flower petals in honor of Cienfuegos on any nearby body of water. I scattered petals on the Río Marañón near my school.

Tyranny Squared

The last decade of freedom in Cuba was ending. Fidel's brand of totalitarian communism was tightening its grip. As Fidel moved Cuba toward the communist bloc, ties with the Soviet Union were getting stronger. Fidel began establishing "people's stores" throughout the island to compete with privately owned retail establishments.

The well-educated knew what communism was and had spoken against it. Now most citizens were questioning where Fidel was taking Cuba. Cubans began to ask one another, "What is communism? What is a communist government?"

Many Cuban socialists, who resided mostly in Havana and who had used the revolution to try to insinuate their agenda into government policy, realized that their utopian, redistribution-of-wealth ideology was leading to the evils of communism, as it usually does. They fled to capitalism—to the United States, to the country so many of them professed to hate. They, like their expatriate counterparts in socialist Europe, continued with the delusion that had their brand of Marxist ideology prevailed, everything would have been OK. They have never acknowledged the part they played in the destruction of their country.

Other utopians, Fabians, and socialists decided to stay and fight. Many of them died or became political prisoners; others finally left on the last commercial flights out of Cuba. Other educated people took a look at what was happening around them and, if they were able, they too fled. *El pueblo*[*] and most middle-class Cubans were left to see Fidel's hand played out and to live the misery he and communism brought to Cuba.

By the end of 1959, a conservative estimate of five hundred Cubans who opposed Fidel's leftist ways were executed in Havana under the direction of Che Guevara, in Santiago de Cuba under Raúl Castro, and throughout the island under other appointed executioners.[30] This was only the beginning. By 1963 Fidel's government had executed 7,720 souls: 2,975 without trials and 4,245 with only mock trials.[31] The number of deaths and disappearances would continue to increase each week, each month, and each year. The numbers would include thousands

---

[*] The masses.

of Cubans killed by the coast guard, when whole families were gunned down while trying to escape the evil regime; Cubans drowned at sea trying to make it to Miami in small craft or by swimming; and those whose disappearances were simply unaccounted for. The number would grow to include landowners—many of whom were the peasants who supported and gave shelter to Fidel in La Sierra. It would grow to include political prisoners who were executed or died from mistreatment or bad conditions in Fidel's jails.

Not counted were the Cubans afflicted with mental breakdowns brought on by shattered lives; Cubans driven to suicide; Cubans whose hearts were broken when they had to choose freedom over family and homeland, often only to face poverty, illness, and unnecessarily early death in the United States; or those whose lives in the United States were ravaged by anger, as were my parents'. Some numbers just don't get counted. The world will never understand the enormity and perfidy of Fidel's destruction of a people. Only a loving God and we, the Cuban people of that time, really understand Fidel's massacre.

No wonder the isolation communism fosters is referred to as the iron curtain. Behind that iron curtain is untold human misery. It is an impenetrable curtain that descends over every front door, every home, and every border and shore in a communist country, smothering light and life.

Yet Fidel's consolidation of power was just beginning.

The republic's last years were gone. My parents' Cuba was gone. They just didn't know it.

1960s

Nine

1960 YEAR OF AGRARIAN REFORM
Año de la Reforma Agraria

At the beginning of 1960, Cuban money still had value. The peso was comparable to the U.S. dollar, but this was about to end.

In 1960, Russia's evil, behind-the-scenes presence came out of hiding in the form of a Soviet diplomat who brought a Russian fair to beautiful, modern Havana. The fair displayed Russian industry, music, books, movies, and plays, all products of Stalin's Russia. For the two weeks the fair ran, the Soviets flooded Havana with all kinds of Russian propaganda, which, quite understandably, didn't show Stalin's atrocities. The Russian fair brought novelty, not quality. At first, Cubans were taken in and fascinated with the Russian products, which did not hold a candle to the quality of Cuban and American products already available in Cuba.

Cubans might not have been so interested in the fair if they had known that Fidel had worked a deal with the Soviets to turn Cuba into a Russian satellite in exchange for his being Cuba's lifetime totalitarian ruler. In early February 1960, Fidel signed an agreement that turned over Cuban interests to the Soviet Union, prostituting her so that he could rule.

The collectivization of Cuba had begun.

In less than a year Fidel managed to confiscate and steal private property from Cubans from all walks of life. He started with the wealthiest and eventually worked his way down to the smallest property and business owners. If you opposed or disagreed with Fidel, your property was confiscated, so confiscation quickly became a tool of political repression.

He nationalized domestic and foreign firms, including large industrial establishments such as textile mills. On behalf of "the public interest," both Cuban-owned and American-owned sugar mills were nationalized, without compensation. The number of American-owned mills was greatly exaggerated by Fidel and widely misunderstood by others who didn't have the facts. In removing the sugar cane industry from the ownership and control of farmers, millers, and other sugar cane professionals, Fidel precipitated a decline in the cane sugar industry of Cuba. The cane sugar industry! Cuba's bread and butter!

Fidel—already having signed over many Cuban rights to the Soviet Union—needed a pretext to break off relations with the United States. In late 1960, Fidel demanded that the United States reduce the staff at Havana's U.S. embassy to the size of the Cuban embassy staff in Washington, DC. As Fidel expected, the United States did not agree and broke diplomatic relations. The U.S. embassy in Havana was closed on January 3, 1961, and the Cuban embassy staff in Washington, DC, was recalled.[32]

Thus, Fidel isolated Cuba from the United States and the rest of the noncommunist world.

The closing of the U.S. embassy was a pivotal moment. A horrific, ill feeling engulfed Cuba. All of a sudden Cubans who had been on the fence, my parents included, were no longer just uncomfortable; they knew that something was very wrong and that something much bigger and worse was coming. They also realized that if you were not on Fidel's side, you were on the wrong side in the government's eyes.

Chaos broke out, with people scrambling to get out of Cuba while there were still commercial flights and freedom to travel. The Cuban exodus had begun, yet this wave was small compared to the mass exodus that would follow the Cuban Missile Crisis.

On the night of December 1, 1960, in direct contradiction to his earlier statements, Fidel admitted he was a communist.[33]

Ten

1961 YEAR OF EDUCATION
Año de la Educación

Life on Calle Fomento was moving forward, or so they thought. My parents' small business was doing well, and my parents were busy remodeling their house. Quality brands and supplies were scarce, but they were still available. As time went by, the word "upgrade" and the idea of fixing anything broken would become extinct; anything that was broken would stay broken forever, for there were no materials to fix anything.

I was three years old and my parents, with their hard work, were still able to give me many of the things they did not have when growing up. Material and sewing supplies were still available for outfits carefully sewn by our seamstress, who lived next door. My sister and I got simple toys for *el Día de los Reyes* (Three Kings Day). Yet within a few years, the celebration of Three Kings Day, because it was related to the birth of Jesus, would be no more. By the early 1970s, there would be no toys to buy. Each child would be given a lottery number on the secular holiday *el Día de los Niños* (Children's Day) to get a small toy provided at a grocery store. If you got one of the last numbers, you got nothing.

In 1961, food was still abundantly available to Cubans at all social levels, the poorest to the richest. No one went hungry in Cuba at that time. If you were hungry, someone would give you a plate of food. That's the way Cubans were. Even Fidel has admitted that Cubans enjoyed a high nutritional standard prior to the full implementation of agrarian and urban collectivization. Afterward, that was not the case.

* * *

On January 1, 1961, a group of approximately nine Cuban exiles returned from Miami under the pretense of getting together with family in Reparto Flores, a suburb of Havana. They were part of the 1,400 exiles who, with training and help from the CIA, were planning to invade Cuba. Their visit was to prepare people. The contacts within Cuba would provide concealment and support of the invasion.

Once again, luck was on Fidel's side. There was an informant at the meeting—one of our own—a Cuban. He left the meeting knowing the entire invasion plan, including the date and time. He carried away a map of the invasion route and a list of the invading exiles' names, as well as their families' names and Cuban addresses. Not long after he left, the house where they met was raided, and the advance guard exiles and their families in Havana and other parts of the island were rounded up by the G-2, Fidel's political police. Additionally, thousands of Cubans—men, women, and children—who were in any way related to the 1,400 invading exiles, were detained in jails, arenas, theaters, and other large buildings. They all were charged with counter-revolutionary activities.

One of our own was the snitch. One of our own was the *chivato*. This *Cuban* man destroyed the last chance for Cuba. Without him, Cuba's long-term fate might have been different. There is an awful irony as well. This mole, this informer, later abandoned Fidel's Cuba and went to live in the United States, repudiating the very regime he had spied on his compatriots for.

Fidel did not know if the exiles in Miami would go ahead with the invasion, but he knew the love of country and the passion for liberty these men felt, so he prepared. He astutely held the captured exiles incommunicado without due process until the actual invasion took place.

After the capture of the Cuban advance guard, U.S. President John Kennedy didn't supply Cuban Brigade 2506 with the fighter aircraft so vital to the invasion's success. He also refused to allow American combat troops to participate in the invasion. The reasons for this depend on which book you read or to whom you speak. One theory is that Kennedy and the CIA decided that since the plans and details were exposed, and Fidel and the Russians were aware of every single invasion detail, it was best to abort the invasion. Others will tell you that Kennedy cancelled American participation because of poor weather.

Did Kennedy and the CIA inform the exiles that they would not have any backup? Some say yes; some say no. Either way, the exiled Cubans decided to carry out the invasion. Either way, Fidel was waiting, like a cat near a mousetrap.

Driven by haste and thinking their fellow countrymen in the area would welcome them as heroes, the Cuban exiles proceeded with the invasion. On April 17, 1961, the exiles set out for *Bahía de Cochino* (the Bay of Pigs), in the southern Matanzas Province. The location was instrumental in the defeat of the mission. The Bay of Pigs is actually not a bay; it is a swamp surrounded by coral reefs known as *dientes de perro*.* The shallow waters and the reefs prevented the exiles' ships from coming close to shore, so they had to anchor a mile out. The landing crafts were rubber rafts, which were torn to pieces on the coral. The exiles thought that local Cubans would support the invasion; however, the area where they landed was a very poor region, largely populated by charcoal workers who were all for Fidel. It was not hard for Fidel to buy the affection of people who had little and lived next to an infested swamp. He had won them over with a few typical, cheap, communist-constructed houses. They thought Fidel was going to change their lives for the better.

Some say that if they were planning a failed invasion, it could not have gone any better than the Bay of Pigs. The invasion was planned with heart and with love of country, but not with brains. Yet in spite of all of the obstacles the exiles faced,

---

* Dog's teeth.

the invasion would have been successful with U.S. air backup, which it did not get.

Unopposed, Fidel's air force flew out to sink the exiles' supply ships while Fidel's army waited patiently and let the exiles land before engaging them with approximately twenty thousand militiamen. The exiles had no supplies, no food, few weapons, and not enough water. Everything that was on the ships was destroyed, and there was no way out. They were trapped in the mosquito- and snake-infested swamp. The exiles were hungry, thirsty, outnumbered, and wounded, yet they fought bravely for two days. Ultimately, the militia came in with heavy artillery and overpowered them.

The day after the fighting ended, Fidel displayed the surviving prisoners in the sports arena in front of television cameras as propaganda for the whole world to see. The atmosphere was tense in Havana. Persecution of anti-Fidel Cubans increased. The G-2 continued rounding up people who were associated with the exiles and *el paredón* was carried out daily at La Cabaña, where the number of executions doubled.

Instead of trying and executing the exiles who participated in the invasion, Fidel held them as ransom, trading them to the United States for tractors and other farm equipment to work the collective farms. The advance guard was not so lucky.

On April 19, 1961, two days after the thwarted invasion, families of eight of the nine advance guard exiles scrambled to get attorneys, having been advised that the exiles were going on trial that very morning. One was still in the hospital after being wounded in the fight. The attorneys rushed to La Cabaña, where so many brilliant minds had been stilled and where now a mass trial of the first advance guard, their families, and a second advance group were being tried, with or without representation.

The outcome was a foregone conclusion. One of the attorneys later told me that the defense attorneys were allowed to see only the indictment. They were not given access to evidence or anything else. There were many charges against the exiles, including counter-revolutionary activities. The trial started at ten in the morning and ran until three the following morning. All defendants were found guilty. Their attorneys decided to appeal. The attorneys were told appeals had to be filed right then and there, and the second decision was rendered immediately. As predicted, the appeal verdict was "guilty."

Sentences were also passed immediately. For the eight advance guard exiles, it was *el paredón*. The rest of the defendants, mostly wives and friends, were given lighter sentences or let go. The condemned exiles were shot within a few hours, early on the morning of April 20, 1961. The leader of the firing squad wanted to shoot the defense attorneys as well; the latter were lucky to escape.

The details of the trial spread rapidly throughout Havana and then throughout the island. The mood was somber.

After the Bay of Pigs, there were smaller invasions and sabotages on other parts of the island, carried out by small groups of Cuban exiles who acted without U.S. backup and whose efforts at rescuing Cuba were futile.

* * *

On May 1, 1961, approximately two weeks after the invasion, Fidel proclaimed victory over American imperialism and reaffirmed that he was a communist[34] and that the revolution was a socialist one. He said that he had not revealed this earlier because it was not convenient, but he had always been a communist.[35] Despite this clear statement, and in an attempt to sugar-coat his agenda, Fidel used and frequently continued to use the word *socialism*, communism's less evil cousin. It is one of his many ways of tricking the utopian idealists of this world into supporting him.

Some take great pride in knowing the difference between Marxism and Leninism. But donkey dung is donkey dung. Marxism, Leninism, communism, Stalinism, and all of their less evil but dark cousins, like socialism, have Marxism at their core. It is the same tree, just different branches. Or think of it as a huge octopus. The big ugly head is Marxism; the huge tentacles are Leninism, communism, and Stalinism. The smaller tentacles with good intentions—but not so good ends—are socialism, utopianism, and redistribution-of-wealth-and-income fanaticism. Their proponents all think they are going to wipe poverty from the face of the earth and, instead, they end up bringing poverty down on everyone. In the end, even the least evil tentacle strangles a society. Not one of them cares about the individual, forgetting that societies are made up of individuals.

Right after revealing he was a communist, Fidel announced that there was no need for free elections and declared the 1940 constitution null and void.

A Day at the Beach, Guarda la Vaca, 1961

Eleven

Emulating other communist leaders who pursued communist hegemony, funded with the gnawing hunger and misery of their people and of the people they conquered, Fidel announced to all Cubans, and to the world, that his goal was to spread communism all over Latin America and Africa.

Autumn 1963 was the fall I started kindergarten at state school Calixto García on the corner of Fomento and Martí.

President Kennedy had hammered the last nail into the coffin. After the Cuban Missiles of October Crisis, as Cuba began to depend more and more on the Soviet Union, *Pravda* wasted no time in announcing that Cuba was one of the socialist countries obedient to the Soviet Union.[36] Fidel confirmed Cuba would be ruled according to the wishes of the Soviet Union.

---

* Fidel designated two years as planning years: 1962 and 1963.

By now, Fidel had nationalized all private schools to establish federal control of education. To succeed in the long run, communism needed a new generation of brainwashed young people to replace their parents, who well remembered their freedom under the republic. With control of education, Fidel turned all schools into centers of communist indoctrination. From that day on, Cuban children were not taught true Cuban history or true world history, but a conglomeration of anti-American, Leninist propaganda. They were taught hate and lies, lies and hate. Our minds were poisoned.

Schools were emptied of college-graduate teachers and were replaced with hastily government-trained, anti-American mouthpieces. Only some math, science, and college Spanish teachers were spared. Schoolbooks were censored. The classics and any true history books were removed and quickly replaced by indoctrination texts with an anti-American theme. Fidel also expelled all academic priests from Havana's Universidad Católica de Santo Tomás de Villanueva.[*] High-quality, balanced education, including the teaching of accurate history, was stolen from Cuban children. Instead, Karl Marx's philosophy of "getting them young" was applied. Government-controlled brainwashing through false education began. Children were denied the right to know.

Libraries were also stripped of all authentic Cuban history books, all true books about the United States, and any book that remotely discussed freedom or justice. Some teachers and librarians were able to smuggle a few books and publications

---

[*] Catholic University of Saint Thomas of Villanueva.

out of the schools and libraries, but most were burned. There were bonfires of books in the center of every city. My city of Holguín was no exception. My parents could see the fires burning in mass rallies at Parque Calixto García.

By the end of 1962, the noose tightened and the communist system was now rock solid in Cuba. The totalitarian government had moved beyond large enterprise to take over many of the medium-sized textile companies, hardware stores, shoe stores, and farms.

The takeover was moving down the economic chain toward us. Soon they would come for the small business that my father and mother had started with such hope in 1958.

The year ended with one of Fidel's tirade speeches, in which he declared that if you did not support the revolution, you didn't have any rights in Cuba. He also declared that the middle class in cities were "parasites."

Lenin became the new Cuban hero, imposed by Fidel on the Cuban people. His pictures were posted on billboards along with Cuba's true heroes and lovers of freedom, such as José Martí* and Antonio Maceo.†

* Cuban poet and national War of Independence hero, 1853–1895.
† Cuban Lieutenant General and War of Independence hero. 1845–1896.

My fifth birthday, 1963

Twelve

Simple Pleasures

As the lights were going out in Cuba, I was an innocent child of six in a comfortable but hardworking, middle-class household. There were few luxuries, but we had our basic needs met. Everything we had was earned and paid for. Yet I was to find out that, even though it took a while to get to me, the darkness was going to swallow us too.

Because my parents had a used car, once in a while we were able to go to the undeveloped Caletones Beach (most Cuban beaches were undeveloped at that time) or to Guarda La Vaca Beach, which had a few plain rental *cabañas.* At that time, all of Cuba's beaches were open and free to any Cuban. People drove or took reliable public transportation to spend a day or more at the beach. Sometimes young people would get together and

---

* Concrete rental units.

rent a bus for a day trip. Occasionally, my sister would invite her girlfriends from school. We would all cram into the car and be off for a day or a night in a simple *cabaña* or in a *casa de huespedes** that didn't have electricity or indoor plumbing. We had no fancy accommodations in upscale hotels, but we had fun.

Another of our anticipated pleasures was Holguín's annual carnival. Cuba was known for its fabulous, colorful Mardi Gras-style carnivals. All major Cuban cities had their own carnival, and people would travel to take part in the week-long festivities. During the day, vendors sold noisemakers, necklaces, and hats to wear at night, when things heated up with high-quality music and dance on an outdoor stage.

In Oriente, Santiago was considered to have the best carnival, but I remember Holguín's as being wonderful too. My father was a member of El Elogio, a men's association, and he served on its carnival committee. Each year our seamstress, who was also a fine designer, designed and sewed gowns for the carnival queen and her court. I remember sitting in her living room watching the fittings. She used only the finest fabrics, and I remember how beautiful they were, especially one in satin the color of buttermilk. Carnival week ended with the biggest parade of the week. It featured many floats; creative costumes; musicians; and dancers, like African rumba dancers. The largest float carried the queen and her court.

Today I hear tourists speak glowingly of Cuba's new carnivals, but in the 1970s my relatives and friends who remained

---

* Boarding house.

in Cuba told me that they bordered on trashy and consisted mostly of loud music and booze. No floats, no beauty, no class. The government even purposely staged these "carnivals" in the courtyards of churches, where drunken carnival goers defiled the church by urinating and defecating on the walls. The decline of the beautiful Cuban carnival tradition is a perfect example of how the Cuban people's culture and history have been swept away.

When my family and I were enjoying ourselves on the beach or at a carnival, my world, along with my family's world and the world of every Cuban, was on the verge of changing in ways no one could have imagined. We did not realize that fifteen years later Cubans would be banned from many of the beaches, including the best, unless they worked in the plush resorts that Fidel built for Canadians and Europeans to draw foreign currency into the country. Fidel stole so much from Cuban children: hope, charity, faith, dreams—even the beaches and the sea.

When I hear Americans, many of them well educated, say that Cuban beaches never belonged to the Cuban people, it just blows my mind. They don't know what they are talking about. From the beginning of the republic up until Fidel Castro took over, the beaches, sand, and oceans were for all Cubans, regardless of social status. Yes, there were fancy houses and private clubs near Havana's beaches. So what? There are fancy houses near the ocean everywhere in the world.

I have learned, through trying to educate them, that these misinformed people cannot be convinced of the truth, so now I just smile that sad smile that has been on my face many times when talking to Americans about the country of my birth. There are so many misconceptions and so much callousness. Many people who pretend to be experts on Cuba condemn the injustice and abuse of Batista and use it as a justification for Fidel, clearly believing Cuba is better off with Fidel, or even that Cubans deserve what they got from him. These so-called believers in justice do not speak of the unfairness of the apartheid society Fidel imposed on Cubans, as exemplified by its dual medical systems and dual levels of access to school supplies, food, basic goods, restaurants, and beaches. My family and I lived it. We know.

Dania Rosa Nasca

Carnival time in Holguín circa 1950's. The
Queen's Float. From author's collection

Just in Time

Not too long after I started school, I ended up at the Calixto García Hospital, weak from infected tonsils and malnutrition. Fidel's destruction of Cuba's excellent health-care system had begun, but in 1964 there were still some good private medical providers. I remember lying on a gurney, my mom standing next to me. A kindly young boy on the next gurney, also with a worried mother, talked gently to me in a caring way, trying to make me feel better. Fidel had not yet extinguished all human kindness in Cuba. Some people still cared about their neighbors.

After receiving an IV, I perked up a little bit, but my tonsils had been intermittently infected for over a year. The chronic infection, combined with the lack of nutrition, was killing me slowly. Food shortages were beginning to occur, but at this point I was malnourished primarily because of my sore throat and because of drainage from the infection, which upset my stomach. I had been in and out of the hospital, enduring very painful injections, which each time would leave me temporarily paralyzed with pain because of the inferior-grade Russian penicillin and how thin I was. My mother decided I needed a tonsillectomy or I would surely die.

She took me to our family cardiologist of many years, Dr. Ramiro Pavón Caballero, who had his *consulta*[*] on the corner of Libertad and Cables. He was a tall, slender man with a pencil-thin, refined mustache and long fingers like those of a classical pianist. He wore impeccable clothing, topped with a starched,

---

[*] Practice; (private doctor's) office.

white-linen lab coat. To me, it seemed that he walked on water. He had the class, refinement, and style that Cubans would soon lose as hunger and scarcity took over. Soon our doctors' professional appearances would disappear, along with their private offices. This doctor's waiting room was very attractive, with white floors of either marble or granite; big, green leather armchairs; and artificial flower arrangements on the tables, all of which comforted and showed respect for the patient.

My mother told the doctor her concern: she was afraid I would not survive the surgery. Knowing the resilience of youth, he told my mother to go ahead with the surgery and assured her that I would not die on the operating table. My father was not so easily convinced, but my mother made the final decision.

On the day of the surgery, my father would not have any part of it. He was afraid I would die.

My mom and I headed for the ear, nose, and throat clinic,* which was a minihospital privately owned by a black doctor (an example of how blacks could advance in pre-Fidel Cuban society). I felt no fear because my great protectress, my mother, was holding my hand. I remember it was around noon; to shield us from the sun, my mom had her umbrella, another needed tool and cultural tradition that would soon become unavailable. The day would come when Cubans could not even replace a broken umbrella to save themselves from the searing noonday sun.

---

* In Cuba, we referred to small hospitals as "clinics," not to be confused with American English meaning of "clinic."

Before the surgery, my mom changed me into my pajamas, which she had brought from home. She walked with me all the way to the operating room. A nice black woman, who was an anesthesiologist or physician's assistant, put a mask over my face. I struggled for a second, and then I was out. The next thing I remember, I was recuperating in the post-op area, which was a plain, small room with a bed and a night table. I spent at least one day in the clinic. The surgeon told my mother my tonsils were like huge, infected tumors. A week later, I was jumping, hopping, and doing all of the active things children do. I was fortunate to get the very last remnants of humane, private medicine in Cuba.

Not too long after Lenin Hospital opened in 1965, Russian and Eastern Bloc doctors arrived in Holguín and in every other city in Cuba as part of the Cuban–Soviet alliance. The well-educated and well-trained pre-Castro physicians who remained in Cuba were informed that the Soviet physicians would demonstrate a better way for them to practice medicine. Little by little, qualified physicians were forced to adopt Soviet procedures or were replaced with new physicians who had been trained by the Soviets.

With the relatively early exodus of so many Cuban physicians and the conversion of medical practices to Soviet procedures and standards, the quality of health care in Cuba plummeted. Ethical, compassionate, and high-quality health care was replaced with communist health care "for everyone," which really meant that there was an apartheid health-care system—one system, subsidized by Russia, for the new elite, high-level communist party members and the occupying Eastern

Bloc families, and a second, vastly inferior system, for everyone else.

The first system would be exported by Fidel as propaganda to poor countries in Africa and Latin America. Decades later on American television, we were still hearing mainstream media reporters bragging with admiration about Castro sending physicians all over the world to bring health care to the poor. The first system is also showcased as Cuba's health-care system when foreigners visit Cuba. Since the 1980s, tourists who become ill are taken to special, plush clinics that are part of the elite system. It is much the same if they have had a bit too much to drink and are a little rowdy and are taken to the clean, relatively comfortable tourist jails and not to the horrendous jails in which Cubans suffer.

The second Cuban health-care system served all but the elite, and it was nothing like the fine medical care that was available to all Cubans before Fidel undermined the system. Little by little, the hospitals where everyday Cubans formerly had received excellent care turned into pigsties with antiquated equipment and few, if any, medications or supplies. "Are you in pain?" was replaced with, "*No diga que duele.*"*

---

* Don't say it hurts.

Thirteen

1965 YEAR OF AGRICULTURE
Año de la Agricultura

Freedom Flights

Regardless of what Fidel named the year, 1965 was known to our family as *El Año de los Vuelos de Libertad*, or the Year of the Freedom Flights. The flights were initiated by the Kennedy–Johnson administration as part of Kennedy's Cuban Missiles Crisis deal with the Soviets, and they were begun under President Johnson. Under the agreement, Cubans wishing to immigrate to the United States would be allowed to leave Cuba and would be flown, at the United States' expense, to the United States, where they would be allowed legal entry.

The average Cuban needed no encouragement to leave Cuba. When Fidel announced that Cubans could apply for the Freedom Flights, a mass exodus began, so deeply unpopular were Fidel and his regime.

To qualify for the Freedom Flights, those wishing to leave Cuba had to have someone in the United States sponsor them. My mother's first cousin in Miami agreed to sponsor my family. Like all potential emigrants, my father went to Havana to apply for Cuban passports for our immediate family—my parents, my sister, and me—which, under the agreement, Cuba would grant. Then he had to obtain our U.S. visas from a third-party embassy. Passage was on a first-come, first-served basis; the earlier the application, the earlier the passage.

The first Freedom Flight took off from Varadero to Miami on December 12, 1965. Between 1965 and 1973, the flights carried more than 265,000 Cubans to the United States.[37]

When the first flights arrived in Miami, Cubans still had their Sunday best clothes and could bring some clothing and personal items. Some of the Cubans, not all, who arrived on the first flights were well-to-do. There is nothing wrong with that. And, yes, a few women wore their mink stoles. In the eyes of many Americans who observed and filmed the first Freedom Flight arrivals, these Cubans did not resemble the immigrants whom the Statue of Liberty welcomed to the United States in the 1800s and early 1900s. The Cubans were clean, not dressed in rags or covered in filth from being on ships.

It was a short flight, not a long ocean voyage, and Cubans had their pride. They were not going to show up in a new country looking terrible. Many Cubans who arrived, even on the early flights, were very ordinary Cubans. Many did not have indoor toilets, but they wore their Sunday best to arrive in their new country, showing respect for themselves and their new land. Thus, they looked more prosperous than they were.

Their arrival was highly televised on the U.S. evening news. An American journalist reported that he did not understand why Cubans were leaving Cuba, for they looked so prosperous. The reporter's broadcast was one of the reasons for the widespread, mistaken idea that only the rich were leaving Cuba. Additionally, the myth of rich Cuban immigrants was propagated in part by Cuban immigrants of modest income telling Americans that they were sugar mill owners and all other kinds of grand lies. Somehow it just stuck that all Cubans who hated Fidel and were able to leave Cuba were rich. This perception did not go unnoticed by Fidel, who played it like a violin to masquerade as a champion of the poor.

What the reporter did not understand was that the first Cubans who arrived on the Freedom Flights were fleeing *what was to come* in Cuba. The hard life and poverty of communist Cuba had not yet changed them in body, mind, and soul. They grasped what Fidel was doing. They did not need to stay and see more. More than a few of these Cubans had relatives who had been executed. Many of these Cubans had been traumatized by Batista, only to be traumatized again by Fidel and again in the United States, where they were misjudged by the American people as they struggled to begin a new life.

Although the Freedom Flights ran until 1973, the media lost interest after the first few. New Cuban immigrants arrived looking worse and worse, but there were no cameras to capture their images. By the time we arrived on April 20, 1970, the cameras were long gone. Although we were not dirty, we were hungry, and many of us were wearing tattered, ill-fitting shoes. Since 1959, every year had taken more of a physical, mental, material, and spiritual toll on the Cuban people. Cubans who left Cuba before 1962 with a full stomach couldn't even imagine what daily life in Cuba had become for those of us who left in 1970, and we would not recognize the misery of Cuba today.

Throughout 1965, while thousands of Cubans flocked to register for visas and a place on the flights, Fidel persisted in the dismantling and ruin of Cuba. The hunger that accompanies communism was rearing up more frequently. Machinery from confiscated private industries was dismantled for parts, which were then sent to Soviet Eastern Bloc countries. The purging of books from schools continued in earnest. More Cubans were being accused of counter-revolutionary activities just for disagreeing with Fidel's regime. Others were accused of working for the CIA and were executed.

People wanted to resist Fidel's government but had no means. They did engage in small acts of defiance when they could.

I remember that availability of goods was becoming erratic. When a supply of wax pens came into stores, the next thing we knew people were writing criticisms of Fidel, including some vulgar jokes, on store windows in town. At this point, such acts were given a pass because the regime was focused on centralizing power and taking over businesses. Later, anyone daring such an act would be spied on, informed on, hunted down, and imprisoned or executed.

Around this time, Miriam, our neighbor Generoso's daughter, got married. Her wedding day is one of my fondest memories. My sister and I were on our way to the wedding, which was being held at one of the alfresco restaurants in Holguín. The bride, all made up and wearing her short wedding veil, looked beautiful, radiant, and joyful. Later, my sister and I went to the lovely but modest reception that was mobbed with friends and relatives. Her father wasn't rich, but he had worked hard all his life and wanted to give and receive the joy of his daughter having a nice wedding.

Not long after Miriam got married, the government closed nearly all restaurants, many of which were alfresco. Without these venues, bridal showers and big weddings were no more. Today, there are plenty of restaurants open in Cuba; however, access to them is restricted to tourists, except for a few that are available to the country's political elite and to Cubans who have American dollars.

Miriam was always very nice to me, even though I was just a little kid. Sometimes I would go over to her house and listen to her sing Beatles songs while she put her sons down for a nap. I always felt so at peace sitting there in her dining room with their shaggy dog walking around and their parrot swinging on its loop. I wondered why I always felt at peace in Miriam's house. Many years later, my mother told me that it was the first home my grandfather built and the first house my mother had lived in.

Miriam, Generoso, and their family left Cuba just before we did. When my mom and I went to their home for *la despedida* (the final farewell), I walked all the way to the backyard where Miriam was hanging laundry.

She said, "Como está, Dania?"

I barely responded. I just smiled and thought, *They, too, are leaving. Everyone is leaving; in time there won't be anyone left.*

Their house—the house my grandfather built, rented, and then sold to Miriam's father—was given to a ranking communist party member. It was not given to one of the poor.

Another Loss

Aunt Zoila, my mother's oldest sibling, lived with my grandparents. On September 26, 1965, she ran the four blocks from their house to ours.

"Papasito is having chest pains," she told us.

My mom and dad got in the car and took my grandfather to Calixto García Hospital. My sister and I stayed home with our aunt. The thought never crossed our minds that Papasito would die. He was going to the hospital and coming back just as he had done before.

Then my sister and I heard my mom screaming from the open windows of our approaching car. She adored her father and she was in shock. She came in the house continuing to scream and crying out, "Papasito is dead!"

I was seven years old, and I was trying to absorb what was going on around me. My aunt slipped out of the house. Being the kindest soul, she took her pain and her loss and quietly went home. It was up to her to tell my grandmother, my uncle, and my other aunt. I later learned that when she got there, she found my Aunt Eva outside buying fruit and vegetables from a vendor for Papasito's return and recovery. (The government had not yet expropriated the little businesses of the street vendors who sold produce.) All of the neighbors ran over to our house. In Cuba most neighbors were like family, always there for you. Fidel had not been able to destroy that yet. Many families on Calle Fomento had known one another for decades, and the children and teenagers had known one another since birth.

The preparations for my grandfather's wake started right away. It would be the customary twenty-four-hour wake at the local funeral home. It was a modest business compared to funeral homes in the United States, but the owners, part of Cuba's strong middle class, were diligent in their work and provided dignified services to Cubans from all walks of life. As Fidel continued the dismantling of Cuba, not even the dead would have any dignity. Fidel would take the deceased back to the boneyard days of colonial times; for now, my grandfather, a simple man who had worked hard all his life, would lie in a simple pine wood coffin and receive a proper burial.

The reception room for the wake was large with a little alcove at its head, where the coffin was surrounded by chairs for the immediate family. My grandfather was in his midseventies when he died. He was an honest and virtuous man, and many friends and family from Holguín and *el campo* came to pay their respects.

My mother decided I also should pay my respects to my grandfather and be able to say good-bye to him. Just before the *entierro,* my father took me to the funeral home. When my mother saw me come in, she came over and carefully and lovingly took me by the hand.

"You must be very quiet," she whispered.

---

* Burial.

She took me to the casket and told me to kiss the glass that was covering Papasito's face. It was not customary to use makeup on the dead in Cuba. Tall and slender by nature, my grandfather looked so old, and his face was so hollow. He had a plain shirt on, a simple shirt for a simple man.

I kissed the glass and said good-bye to my beloved grandfather. In later years, my mom would talk about how much he loved me and how I was his favorite.

I went around the casket and sat down next to my grandfather's sister. How she cried for her brother! Families were so close back then. She had the bluest eyes, and to me her tears seemed to be a stream. I remember thinking, *I have never seen tears pour out of someone's eyes quite that way*. I just sat there, looking at her.

After a bit I got restless, as any child would, and moved around and looked out into the salon. The funeral home was mobbed, packed with generations of family and friends getting ready for the procession to the cemetery. My father took me home before the procession started. Although I was not taken to the cemetery, I will be forever grateful to my mom and dad, who had the wisdom to take me to the wake, if only for half an hour, to say good-bye to Papasito.

It is painful that this was the only time my mom would be present for a member of her family's last hours. It is so very important and healing for the human heart to be with your loved ones at the end of their earthly lives, be there at their deathbeds, tell them you love them, pay your respects, be present at their wakes, and bury them. My mother would lose that healing gift forever when we left Fidel's Cuba.

Almost immediately after my grandfather's burial, I noticed a change in my grandmother's home. The little bit of joy that had come back into their house after my uncle's suicide drained away. The sorrow and despair that returned to that house never again moved out.

I have some wonderful recollections of Papasito. I vaguely remember *La Noche Buena*, Christmas Eve dinners, which we celebrated at my grandparents' house. We always had *lechón asado*,[*] white rice, black beans, and *casabe*.[†] When I got bored, Papasito would take a rocking chair out to the front porch. There I would sit on his lap, and we would count the cars going by. Gradually, the number of cars going by became fewer and fewer. Eventually, only an occasional government vehicle would pass. I wondered where all of the cars had gone. I was too young to realize that Fidel was bringing Cuba to a halt.

My memories of my grandfather are wonderful because I remember his presence and love, and they are sad because his face has become fuzzy in my mind's eye. Without a photograph, I can't remember how he looked. I am also sad when I remember how unnecessarily difficult his life became in his last years.

Before Papasito's death, Fidel's totalitarian government began turning off the electricity after dark and cutting off running water after a certain time in the afternoon. Even at age six, I asked myself what sense it made. Later, after shortages became real and acute, I realized it was to get people accustomed to the shortages to come—accustomed to a way of life that would get

---

[*] Roast suckling pig.

[†] Manioc cake.

worse every day, accustomed to government tactics for breaking the human spirit. It was all about demeaning and degrading. It was a way of systematically breaking down people in the cities, where there were large concentrations of people, until they felt helpless, totally docile, and dependent on the government. It was a means of control. It was a way of getting people accustomed to constant misery and privation.

I remember my grandfather, a man in his seventies, a man with angina pectoris, walking four blocks from his house to ours with two buckets to get water from our *aljibe.* The *aljibe* was the sophisticated catch-water system that he had put in many years before when he had built the house we lived in. The system included a copper chute that directed rainwater off the roof into the cistern after it passed through a copper filtering system. When the cistern was full, the chute could be closed. The water was crystal clear and could be used for everything, including drinking. I remember my grandfather standing by the reservoir with one foot resting on the cement ledge around it. He was wearing his good brown shoes. I am glad he wore his good shoes, for he did not have many more steps left to take. Sometimes we save things for a special occasion, not realizing that the special occasion is right then and there.

The cistern was a blessing for us, for our extended family, and for the neighbors on our street. Papasito never thought of building an *aljibe* for their new modest house on Cervantes because, by then, every house in the city had running water.

---

* Underground cistern to catch rainwater.

How could Papasito have known that one day they would again need a private water supply?

Not long before my grandfather died, my mother got fabric to have new shirts made for him. She so adored her family. She was very generous and loved helping them and bringing them joy. We took Papasito in our car for his measurements at a tailor shop, which, like many small Cuban businesses, was located in a private home. The front of the house had been turned into a work space. There were scissors, bobbins, spindles, measuring and cutting tables, and Singer sewing machines. I was fascinated by the new experience and took a little walk around the room just to get a better look.

Papasito's tailor was just one example of a country of industrious Cubans with high work standards. Whether they were self-employed or they worked for someone else, Cubans were hard workers. There was so much knowledge, craftsmanship, and talent in Cuba. These craftsmen and artisans were not as wealthy as many in the world would lead you to believe, but their businesses put food on the table.

My grandfather would not live to wear his new shirts. He died before they were ready. Looking back, I am thankful that my grandfather died while urban Cubans could still find food. There were shortages, but stores still had some supplies, and products and rationing had not yet been fully implemented. Life was still good in many ways, and hunger had not yet engulfed the cities. Papasito was also blessed that he died before he had to say good-bye to us and before my uncle and grandmother had to turn all of the family land over to the government.

Just before my grandfather died, he had a great crop on his farmland. He paid all of his debts and had a small profit, some of which he distributed equally among his children. A few days after paying his creditors and his workers and after thanking God aloud that he did not owe a penny to anyone, he died.

My grandfather was good to his family and to his fellow man in general. He had lost a son, his smartest son, and yet he did not grow bitter. He owned a little land so he could grow sugar cane and make a living. He was a man who always had a kind response when others were not so nice.

My grandfather was a good man. He was blessed that he died before Fidel had his full way with Cuba.

La Novena

After Papasito's burial, we began *La Novena*, a tradition rooted in the Catholic faith—nine consecutive days of prayer for my grandfather. My grandmother's house was packed with family and friends who gathered in the evenings to recite the rosary. I had never heard so many people say the rosary in complete unison. It made a profound impression on me. I thought it was the most beautiful and unifying thing I had ever heard.

The rosary and the novena were two of many beautiful Catholic traditions that would soon disappear from Cuba as people became afraid to gather for spiritual purposes or even to practice their faith in their own homes. Although surely some individuals continued to pray the rosary in private, where no one could see them, novenas and other traditional group expressions of faith outside a church building ceased to exist, for they were forbidden by the government.

As is documented in old newsreels, in 1962, when I was four, Fidel persecuted and expelled from Cuba all foreign and most domestic nuns. The few Cuban nuns who stayed understood that they had to live very quiet lives and not rock the boat. The first time I saw a nun was when I came to the United States in 1970.

Aida was Papasito's rosary lead. She had a deep Catholic faith. Educated by nuns, she heard God's true call to dedicate her life to Christ by becoming a nun; however, when Fidel closed all private schools and most monasteries and convents, Aida's dream of serving in the church was shut down. How could she evangelize or even minister in the name of the church when religion was not allowed outside church walls?

Aida was not able to leave Cuba because she had elderly parents who were too old to uproot, and she needed to stay to take care of them. Aida told everyone that she would become a nun in her heart. She took a self-imposed oath of celibacy and prayer. An oath of poverty was not necessary; Fidel would take care of that. Although she was not able to wear the habit she longed to, her wardrobe was simple. She wore only plain white, gray, or black clothes and plain, closed black shoes. She always had a simple haircut and wore no makeup whatsoever—all so very much like a nun. I remember my mother speaking of Aida with great respect and admiration. I wonder what a difference Aida could have made in people's lives had Fidel not interfered with and limited her vocation.

The Cemetery

Holguín's main cemetery was, and is, at the very end of Luz Caballero. After my grandfather died, going to the cemetery became a weekly routine. Paying respects and taking care of the family grave were very much a part of Cuban culture.

My very first trip to the cemetery was with my mom. Like most seven-year-olds, for me every new experience was a mystery and full of suspense. As soon as we crossed Cervantes, I realized I was in unknown territory. I didn't remember ever being this far away from home on foot.

To get to the cemetery, we walked down our street and made a right turn by Caridad's house onto Luz Caballero. As soon as we got close to the *tintorería** on the corner of Luz Caballero and Cervantes, I could hear the industrial steam iron pressing down on garments. Then, a wonderful steamy smell drifted out to the street. Like the tailor, the owners of the *tintorería* lived behind the store.

We also walked by the *carnicería*† on the corner of Luz Caballero and Fomento. When we first started our weekly walks, it was a viable business. Two years later, when I was nine, it was government owned and government run to sell the meager amount of poor-quality meat that was rationed by the government. Then, on *el día de carne* (meat day), the store would become a hellish place, with lines of housewives fighting over a scrap of beef or a chicken that surely looked two ounces bigger than the one next to it. The butcher had to have nerves of steel.

---

* Dry cleaners and laundry.
† Butcher shop.

But, on our early walks to the cemetery, we didn't know any of that was to come.

On that first trip, Luz Caballero and the walk seemed endless. Then, straight ahead, I saw a huge, bright yellow, mission-style wall. I had never seen a cemetery before, and I was fascinated. As we got closer, I could see a big iron gate.

Before we went in, we stopped at the florist across from the cemetery. The florist shop was another family owned small business. It was not much bigger than a walk-in closet, but there were roses and all kinds of flowers in cone-shaped containers. For a few cents, my mother bought flowers for my grandfather. Sometimes she would buy flowers for our house too. I loved the visits to the cemetery with stops at the florist, and my mom loved to buy flowers for her dad. She was as good to him in death as she was when he was alive. I learned the names of different kinds of flowers, and I enjoyed taking the newspaper that the flowers were wrapped in and making a thick ball to clean dry leaves and petals off the top of the tomb.

We always went into the cemetery by the main gate. On the inside of the front wall, there were niches that were the oldest tombs in the cemetery, their inscriptions worn away by time and weather. My mom told me that they were the graves of the first Spanish settlers.

We walked a little farther. When we got to the second gate, there was a *panteón** tucked in the corner between the gate and the wall. When open, that second gate almost embraced the grave as if to protect it. There we turned left and immedi-

---

* Grave in the form of an above-ground vault.

ately passed a family grave that in five years would welcome the sweet, innocent body of my schoolmate, Verena, who would become a victim of Fidel's "voluntary" farm work for high school students.

Finally, after going up a few steps and a bit farther, we arrived at our family plot. All tombs in the cemetery were built above ground due to Cuba's heavy rains. The graves were surrounded by a big rectangular enclosure, which was typically at least five feet by six feet. The enclosures were made out of a durable stone, such as granite, marble, or limestone. Some of the tombs had crosses and others had statues. Some were opulent and others were simple. Families built family plots according to their means. If a family had a lot of money and they wanted to spend it that way, why not? If someone, like our family, could not afford marble, there were other, less expensive but serviceable stones available.

Almost immediately after my grandfather died, my mother went to a stone worker, also located near the cemetery, to have the grave book made. Grave books were very heavy stones in the shape of a book that became the deceased's headstone. My uncle Valito's grave book was already there. For my grandfather, my mother chose a stone that had a removable flower vase in the back. Like many headstones, it contained the name of the deceased; birth and death years; and, as always, "Rest in Peace."

One memory that warms my heart is truly magical because I saw it through the eyes of a child. I remember my mother reciting the profession of faith aloud. When she got to the part, "He (meaning our savior, Jesus) will come again to judge the living and the dead," I would picture all of the dead people sitting up in unison and rising from the crypts.

Being multigenerational graves, the tombs were built to last many lifetimes. On top there was a very heavy slab with huge iron handles that covered a big opening, the actual grave. Usually people in the same family died spaced out over time, so there was enough time between burials for the tomb to accommodate other relatives' remains. On the death of a family member, a cemetery worker would lift the heavy top slab and, to make room for the newly deceased, would rake the previous remains into a niche in the back of the tomb where they would reside with those of their ancestors. Families washed and repaired family tombs on All Saints Day, which Cubans call *el Día de los Muertos.* The roots of this custom were both respect and the practical need of keeping the tombs in good repair.

When communism's grip tightened, and families began to leave Cuba in huge numbers, the graves were no longer maintained. Just as Fidel's actions would result in the crumble and collapse of every element of Cuba's infrastructure, every city and every farm, so would the cemeteries and the tombs of our ancestors collapse into disrepair.

The florist and stone worker would not be spared in the takeover of privately owned businesses. With the collectivization of the stone workers, Fidel destroyed yet another artisan craft, illogically assigning them jobs that did not require special skills. This one trade had supported the construction and repair of fine buildings, cemeteries, and churches. In the takeover,

---

* Day of the Dead.

Fidel broke the long association between artisans and family burial and between artisans and the church. By the time Pope John Paul II planned his visit to Cuba in the late 1990s, most churches were in dire need of repair. Fidel had to bring crews from Europe to repair them. How sad! Before Fidel, the talent, know-how, and materials for building and repairing houses, schools, and churches were right there in Cuba.

It was not customary in Cuba to build a family plot before you needed it. Families who had built plots before Fidel came into power were lucky, for they could bury their dead with dignity. After approximately 1966, if you did not have a *panteón*, when you died you were put in the ground and dirt was thrown on you. No one could build a family plot for his or her loved ones because materials and skills were not available.

Fidel Robs the Dead

One day, a few years after my grandfather died, my mother got a letter from the cemetery asking her to come to a meeting. During the meeting, cemetery officials, who were new government employees, asked family plot owners to share their family plots with nonfamily because the cemetery was running out of room.

I wonder how many people around the world who praise Fidel would like to have their loved ones' graves opened and have a stranger's remains thrown in with them? Respectful burial of the dead is a hallmark of civilization; it distinguishes human beings from animals. My mother, typical of her, spoke up and told them that there was plenty of room and that more family *panteones* could be built had Fidel not taken away the means and the materials.

Prior to Fidel, mass burial had been forbidden by the republic. Later, as the iron grip of totalitarian communism tightened on Cuba, the dead were thrown in nameless mass graves, with quick decomposition encouraged. Who could have imagined this indignity?

Yet on reflection, it is logical. Fidel took dignity away from the living. Why wouldn't he take it away from the dead?

Fourteen

Fidel instituted another "unifying" phase. All high school students had to do mandatory *trabajo voluntario*. Yes, mandatory volunteer work! The "voluntary" wording was to fool the world, most especially the American media. It was not long before international media started reporting the lie that Cuban children eagerly volunteered for the good of the country.

Students were taken from their homes and sent away for several weeks during the school year to do farm work on the new collective farms. The choice was very clear: do the mandatory volunteer work and be allowed to continue your education or be forced to drop out of high school.

The real purpose of the mandatory camps was not farm work; it was to make sure that when your children came back—if they were lucky enough to come back alive—they were no longer your children, but children of the state. The farm camps were a tool to rob youth of all the values and decency passed on to them by their parents. In these camps, there were no Sunday religious services. In addition to lack of respect for religion, there was a lack of respect for family and human life. By the early 1970s, rooms in these camps were purposely made coed to encourage premarital sex. The number of abortions increased radically, and the farm camps even had clinics on site where abortions were performed. A generation was being reshaped into a society very different from that of its parents.

My mother intuited the truth. She recognized the camps as a way of brainwashing her children and changing them into comrades and into the new class that Fidel was working to create. Since we were leaving the country on a Freedom Flight, my mother decided my sister was not going to the farms. On registration night, my mom, my sister, and I walked to the high school on Calle Martí. We went up to the desk.

"I am Mari's mother, and I am here to inform you that my daughter is not going to farm camp," my mother said clearly and directly.

"We will take good care of her," said the teacher, who was a red-haired woman with a gentle way about her and a smile that seemed to say, "I am sorry it has come to this."

"She is not going," my mother reiterated, and we walked out.

Once the high school students left to work on the collective farms, it did not take long for the horror stories to get back. Farmers had worked the land for generations and knew the precautions they had to take with fertilizer, but teachers and students didn't. Not knowing farming techniques and lacking tools, they spread fertilizer with their hands. After a long day of work, which most of them were not accustomed to, they were hungry. Not having proper hand-washing facilities available to them, they ate whatever was given to them with hands that had a residue of cow manure. Their food became tainted with manure, and soon many of them became victims of salmonella poisoning. Throughout Cuba, many students and teacher chaperones died, their lives unnecessarily shortened. The world never knew.

As I listened to the stories that were coming back with the students, I wondered what was going to happen to me if we didn't leave Cuba before I was of high school age. Even today when I hear about mandatory community service in exchange for college financial aid or as a requisite for graduation, it sends chills up my spine.

Even though I was only eight years old, I was beginning to understand. I could see that bad things were happening, and my mother helped me to understand that I was already living in an altered Cuba. I heard the adults talking about how the government had closed the private schools, had removed true teachers from public schools, and had burned true Cuban history books about liberty, freedom, and democracy in the Western Hemisphere, along with any books revealing the evils of communism.

Now the schools were more accurately termed centers of indoctrination. Even as a young child who liked to learn, I found everything was gray and boring in Fidel's "free-education-for-everyone" schools. Beyond reading, writing, and some sciences, nothing much was taught besides a distorted communist version of history. There were no art lessons and no music lessons, except for songs with anti-American lyrics. The privilege of studying the arts was reserved for a few of the smartest children of high-ranking party members and occupying forces, who were allowed to attend the elite communist schools. Had my parents bought the piano that my mother so wanted for my sister when we left Cuba, it would not have gone to a public school. It would have been given to one of the elite-only schools, or even more likely, to an elite family.

At this point, it should be noted that not all communists belonged to the new communist elite; only a few at the very top of the regime were among the elite class. Yes, a doctrine that preaches elimination of social classes and leveling of wealth ended up making most of the population poor while creating a separate class of its own social and economic elite.

Justice Fidel-Style

On a typical hot, humid day in 1966, my father was behind the counter of our family business, La Quincalla. A "useful idiot," someone who is used by communism but does not know its end results, entered the store.

"Would you like to buy beef?" he asked my father.

"I don't buy illegal beef," my father answered him, intuitively realizing it was a trap. Strike one against the government.

After the agrarian law and food rationing were imposed, it became illegal for any cattle farmer to kill a cow and sell the beef, even though the cow was his property. Only the government could slaughter cattle and sell meat through the rationing system. My father's quick answer was an attempt to put an end to any future tricks. It was good, quick thinking.

After closing the shop as he did every midday when the intense heat became unbearable and people stayed inside for a couple of hours, he told my mom about the man who came into the shop. She agreed that it was a trap. They both thought that was the end of that. They were wrong. As my father was about to find out, evil doesn't give up very easily. The devil is persistent.

A few days later, the militia showed up during business hours. They told my father they wanted to question him. When the police came for you, you didn't dare ask why; you simply went quietly so as not to ruffle any feathers. One tried to give the impression of cooperation.

I wasn't home when they took my father away to the interrogation room of the local police station. His only "crimes" were legally applying to leave the country and declining to buy beef clandestinely. He later told us that the police sat him down, surrounded him, and the inquisition began.

The interrogators—all Cubans—were recent graduates of the Russian and Eastern Bloc school of interrogation, torture, and suppression of human rights. They were the new Cuban comrades sent to Russia and Eastern Europe to learn the impose-the-regime-no-matter-what techniques. Some were brainwashed, and some simply enjoyed the new power they had been given. Either way, they were brutal and had no problem inflicting psychological and physical pain on their countrymen.

The interrogation started. The objective was for my father to admit he had done something illegal so they could detain him.

"On such-and-such date, a man entered your business and asked if you would buy clandestine beef," said one of the interrogators.

"Yes, he did, and I told him that it was illegal and that I was not interested," my father answered.

Strike two.

They were hoping my father would lie so they could accuse him of lying. They changed their tactics. One interrogator turned to another. "Call so-and-so and tell him to go to this man's house and take his car." My father continued to deny that he did anything illegal.

The interrogator turned around and shouted, "Go to his house and take his business away."

Still my father denied wrongdoing. He knew he was there because he had applied to leave the country. To the Fidelistas, this made him a *contrarevolucionario.**

"I am leaving the country due to Fidel Castro's announcement that we could do so on the Freedom Flights. I haven't done anything illegal," he told them.

Strike three.

The main interrogator was desperate. They had to make him say he did something illegal, and my father was not budging.

"Where are your two daughters? Where is your wife?"

It had been an exhausting, mentally grueling day for my father. He had been there for hours. He was tired, thirsty, and hungry, and now afraid for his family.

---

* Counter-revolutionary.

"A few years ago, I bought beef on the black market to feed my family," my father blurted out. He wasn't a marine trained not to break during interrogation. He was just an ordinary husband and father trying to protect his family.

A diabolical smile of victory slowly overtook the faces of the investigators, especially the lead one.

"You are free to go home," said the main investigator.

My father went home and told my mother the whole story. Cubans bought food and other goods on the black market all of the time. It was the person who sold on the black market who was most likely to get in trouble, usually not the buyer. My father thought they would leave him alone now. He was wrong.

A few days later, the *milicianos*[*] came and arrested my father, charging him with illegal purchase of beef. He would have to stand trial.

Although not all of the people who applied for Freedom Flights were targeted for such harassment, some of them were. Envy and revenge come in many forms. Perhaps someone who was unable to leave was lashing out. In my father's case, perhaps someone who had little and was poor and powerless before Fidel's regime took over wanted revenge against someone who did have something, not realizing my father had once been poor too. Maybe it was random.

My father was taken to the fire station on Luz Caballero, which had been turned into a jail. When my mother took me to see my father, I saw that the building had been built before Fidel, because it was a modern, well-built structure, an example

---

[*] Militiamen

of the republic's many accomplishments. Everything Fidel built was notable for the inferior materials and poor workmanship.

I remember the fire truck from this station driving down our street, wailing its sirens. What an exciting feeling that was for me, running after the fire truck with the other kids. One day, like everything that was bright and colorful and served a good purpose, the fire truck disappeared; I never saw it again.

My father was not a dangerous prisoner, so they brought him out to the entrance. I was able to wave at him, but when I made an attempt to get closer, the guard signaled me to stay put.

As we were getting ready to leave, a prisoner flew a paper plane from one of the upper windows. The same guard walked away from the building and looked up to see if he could see who did it. I did not like the look on his face. I remember thinking, *My God, it was only a paper plane.* That moment was ground zero for me. Right then and there, young as I was, I felt the ire of injustice and knew we were living under an evil government.

Future attempts to take me to see my father before the trial were futile. I cried, screamed, and refused to go. I guess it was my way of dealing with the injustice of it all. My sister and mother were allowed to visit him for a few minutes now and then, and they learned that the prisoners had to sleep on the floor. Only guards got cots.

While my father awaited his trial, his brother and my oldest aunt helped my mother run the business. Everyone pitched in to keep it going while he was away. The inventory was small, and the quality of the products was lower than before. The American embargo affected goods available in Cuba, but even

Dania Rosa Nasca

if there had been no embargo, products from the United States would not have made it to our store. Quality goods that still came in from Spain, one of the countries that did not break relations with Cuba, went to restricted access stores, not to average Cuban stores like ours. Only the new elite and the Eastern Bloc were worthy. Despite these impediments, my mother became quite a businesswoman.

The Trial

My father's trial began.

By this time, all attorneys had been forced to take a course in Marxist law, which was really no law at all. My father was given a government attorney; he was not a public defender, but he was an attorney who knew that, no matter what he said, my father would be found guilty.

Adult family members were allowed to attend the trial. Oh, how I wish I had been able to go. My mother and Grandmother Cuca (my father's mother) went to the trial together. My grandmother was holding a small statue of the Virgin Mary hidden inside her purse. She was holding it very tight, she later told me. My mother came home, and in her articulate and outspoken way, recounted the details of the trial to anyone who wanted to listen. My mom was eloquent. When she talked, you got her point.

"There were five defendants sitting at the defendants' table," she said. "Your father had his hands folded in front of him on the table. One defendant was wearing one of your father's shirts. He did not have a shirt to wear to the trial, so your father gave him one of the ones I had taken over to the jail."

Nothing could have prepared my mother, my grandmother, and the relatives of other defendants for the embarrassing insults they received. The trial turned into a stream of degrading slurs spewed at the wives of the men on trial, all of whom had applied to leave on the Freedom Flights.

"These women," the district attorney started, "are leaving the country to sell their bodies on the streets of the United States." He was calling them prostitutes!

The women in the courtroom blushed crimson, but no one could say or do anything. There was no getting up and leaving. They had to take the insults for the sake of their loved ones and out of fear for their own lives. The trial truly showed that my father and the other defendants were there for one, and only one, reason—they were leaving the country, so the regime wanted to discredit and humiliate them.

Finally, the lies and insults from the Cuban district attorney ended. The mock trial was over. All were found guilty. Sentences would be passed in private on another day. Relatives would not learn the sentences until they visited their loved ones in jail.

The Crusade

My mom was determined that they were not going to sentence my father to any jail time. She set out on a crusade that took the two of us to many high-ranking Cuban communist officials' homes. She started out by finding the names and addresses of these government officials. I have no idea how she did that, but she did.

"Today you are not going to school," she told me. I was delighted. We were off to fight our crusade for justice.

At each house, she would knock on the door and ask if she could speak to the official. They all received us. She would wait until we were seated in their living rooms to tell them what her visit was all about. Then she would start her plea. She would tell them the whole story in detail. She stated that my father was innocent, and she would appreciate it if they would intervene in any way they could so he would not get a jail sentence and could come home. When she was done, she thanked them and off we went to the next house.

It is fair to say that these officials were not stupid. They could see what was going on in Cuba: food shortages, political and religious persecution, people disappearing left and right, spying, snitching, indoctrination, humiliation, unjustified incarceration, seizure of private businesses, humane medicine slowly becoming a thing of the past, and—hanging over it all—growing despair. They even may have disagreed with what was happening, but they were people who had already sworn solidarity with Fidel. Even if they wanted out, they knew trying to separate themselves from the party could mean death.

Would my mother's crusade pay off? Would they let my father go free? (We would have settled for house arrest.) My mother convinced herself that my father would not get any jail time.

The Sentence

The day my father received his sentence, my mother and grandmother went to visit him. They were sitting in the waiting room and could see the stairway leading to where my father was being held.

"He came down the stairs, smiling, trying to make it look like nothing was wrong. He was trying to make it easier on us," my grandmother later told me.

"I have been sentenced to one year in jail," my father told them.

I truly believe my father was lucky that he only got a one-year sentence. If it had not been for my mother's intervention, he could have easily received ten years or more. Nevertheless, my mother and grandmother were devastated. They left and went separate ways. My grandmother went straight to the bus stop and took a bus home.

My mom just wasn't ready for the news. She went directly to her mother's house, her refuge. She went straight to my grandmother's bedroom and cried and cried about the injustice. I came running to see what was wrong. She was hysterical. They were both sitting on my grandmother's bed. I remember that my mom was still wearing *ropa de luto** in observance of my grandfather's death.

My mom was letting it all out. Fidel and the communist regime were called every name in the book. I was sure the communist witches next door were listening, just like I was sure they knew my father's sentence way before we did. My grandmother was silent; supportive in the silence that comes from the wisdom of old age. She knew there was no consoling her daughter.

---

* Mourning clothes. After the death of an immediate relative, Cuban women only wore plain or print black, white, or gray clothing for a year to show they were in mourning.

I was standing there trying to take all this in. I was not too young to learn how to despise; nor was I too young to see injustice and understand it for what it was. I could see what human beings can do to other human beings for the sake of power, or belonging, or out of just plain meanness. I was not too young to see evil for what it was.

My paternal grandfather died in Cuba in 1971, before he got the *salida* (permission to leave). Grandma Cuca, however, was able to leave on the Freedom Flights after his death. Many years later in the States, she told me, "People just don't know how evil Fidel is." My grandmother never went to school, but hers was the voice of experience and common sense. People do not have to be educated to know and speak the truth.

I became very good at dissimulating. I learned to be careful about what I said and did. Like so many others, I had already learned how to recognize communists by how they talked and walked. I learned how they carried out the indoctrination that they had received from the government. I learned how quickly they turned on you and how quickly they intimidated people. I learned what they would do to friends, neighbors, and at times even their own families. I learned to spot the government spies dressed in regular street clothes, seeing how they held their cigarettes, pretending they just happened to be on a corner or in a crowd smoking or just looking out the window. It was a scary thing to see.

Communist party members were walking mouthpieces. It was a sad and scary thing to see how people became instruments; useful idiots of malice and deception. They did not think. If you said something not in alignment with the party line or expressed an opinion, the person next to you or some-one nearby, who was listening without your knowing it, would lash out at you and give you a revolutionary communist lec-ture. It happened in less than a second.

Brainwashing and irritability from hunger ruled. Yes, the same political correctness that ruled in Russia when Stalin imposed communism with the barrel of a gun was now being imposed on Cuba. *You can't say this. You can't say that. If you think it, don't say it. It may very well land you in jail or worse.* This may seem an extreme statement, but if you had lived it, you would understand.

Visiting Hours

My father was sent to a jail just outside Holguín. My mom took me to see him. A multitude of people were waiting, trying to visit their loved ones. As my mother began to talk to others outside the jail, I learned that some of their relatives were in jail because they had said something negative about Fidel or had tried to fight the totalitarian system. Others were in the same boat we were; their relatives were in jail because they had applied to leave the country.

When we finally got in, I saw a huge field of folding chairs laid out in rows. Some prisoners were playing guitar and putting on a talent show for the families. I was standing by my father, who was sitting on one of the chairs. *Be strong, be strong,* I keep saying to myself. *Don't cry, don't cry.* But tears at the injustice began to flow, and I could not stop them. *I hate communists,* my tears screamed.

My grandmother, my mother, and my sister went back to visit several times, but I would not go. They would get up very, very early to leave at dawn. Leaving early when it was cooler made the trip and the wait in line at the jail somewhat more comfortable. Just because I didn't go didn't mean that I didn't hear the stories when my mom got home. I am grateful she didn't hide things from me. I am grateful she told me the truth. Parents don't always protect their children when they hide the truth from them.

Prisoners were divided into five dorms in five sections of the prison: section one was for the best-behaved inmates, all the way up to section five, which housed the worst of the worst.

When our neighbor Fermin and his family left Cuba, they left a big, well-built colonial house behind. I remember going to their house for their daughter's birthday parties. Because the house was very spacious and had two front entrances, the government divided the house into a duplex. A black *miliciano*, who was a guard at the prison, and his family were given one of the duplex units. This black *miliciano* was tall, communist, and hungry. I imagine he had a lesser house but more food before Fidel.

It seemed to me that the lights went out in that house as soon as they split it; it never looked or felt the same to me. But then the lights were going out all over Cuba as the darkness descended in ever more smothering waves.

The guard, who had been indoctrinated to hate those who were leaving Cuba, recognized my father in section one of the prison.

"What are you doing here?" he asked, looking at my father with hatred. He promptly switched my father to section five. He had no justification; he had just been trained to hate.

Along came another prison guard, who either had a heart and a sense of fairness or knew how to run a prison properly. Knowing my father was a well-behaved prisoner, he said to him, "What are you doing here?" and he sent my father back to section one.

This power struggle between the two prison guards went on and on, with my father being sent back and forth between sections one and five like a pawn in a chess game until the better man won. Ultimately, my father was left in section one. For once, truth and justice prevailed in a Cuban prison. My father, who did not deserve any imprisonment, was at least put in the better part of the prison.

The conditions in the prison were terrible, though, even in section one. They only fed the prisoners the minimum number of calories needed for survival. One day, they lined up the prisoners and told them to get their tin cups; they were getting *dulce de fruta bomba* (papaya fruit in syrup). The prisoners were very excited because they were so hungry. They could almost taste it. Surely they would get a cup or half a cup. When my father's turn came, the guard put the equivalent of three pieces of fruit cocktail in his tin cup. My father turned to the inmate behind him and poured his share into the inmate's cup and walked away. It was a matter of principle. He did not want communist "generosity." It was an insult to his dignity.

These were just a couple of incidents. The stories came in a steady stream. My mom made sure she told everyone she could, so they would know the unfairness of the system.

This was a very difficult time for my father and our family, but it needs to be said that, even though my father's incarceration and treatment in prison were great injustices, they were mild compared to the way Fidel's regime has treated political prisoners. Cuban political prisoners, held in Isla de Pinos and other equally horrible prisons, consisted largely of intellectuals, attorneys, journalists, dentists, doctors, teachers, professors, writers, architects, scientists, and engineers. Good men and women; they were the brightest of the bright. Some fought with Fidel in the Sierra, and almost all supported him until they realized he was leaning toward communism. As early as 1966, news spread from family to family and province to province about the mistreatment of Fidel's foes in prison. Word leaked out that prisoners were being subjected to terrible prison conditions, denied medical care, starved, and mentally tortured, including being forced to hear the executions of fellow inmates. These abuses led to prison deaths from disease, suicide, and even murder, raising the death toll beyond deaths by execution.

As a child, I heard snippets of the stories from my mom, but it wasn't until many years later that I ventured to find out more about Fidel's betrayal of his friends and his one-time supporters and about his unconscionable treatment of prisoners. It wasn't until I read their testimonies[38] that I truly understood. It would take many more years for me to understand that Marxist regimes always eliminate their brightest and most successful citizens first, because they are the ones who can bring others into the light, they are the ones who are capable of fighting the encroaching darkness by bringing the light of truth. Those with the light of knowledge and truth are the most dangerous to regimes that breed and feed on ignorance, darkness, and lies.

The Second Crusade

My mom heard about *La Granja*, a system of prison farms where prisoners were held in bunkhouses instead of cells and where they worked the land. The *Granjas* were completely different from the regular prisons. Thousands and thousands of Cubans who were caught trying to escape Cuba, and Cubans who, like my father, were being punished for having applied to leave the country legally, were now being sent to the *Granjas*. In the *Granjas*, the food was better than in regular jails, and the prisoners had more freedom to move around. They were responsible for keeping their bunkhouses clean, making their beds, and doing their own laundry. They also worked in the kitchen and did the cooking.

"Today you are not going to school," my mom again said, and once again I was delighted.

Off we went, from one communist party member's house to another, for my mother to plead my father's case, this time for his transfer to *La Granja*. In many cases, they were the same houses we had visited before. Once again, we would sit down in the officials' living rooms. My mother would make her request, thank them for listening, and tell them she appreciated anything they could do. On and on we went. Everyone received us. I truly believe these party members were good people caught in a bad situation.

Mom's efforts paid off. My father was transferred to a work farm. It was in the province of Oriente, where we lived, but closer to Bayamo, a nice city very much like Holguín, with the same huge colonial houses built in the Spanish architectural style. Visiting day came, and my mom, sister, and I took the bus to see my father. His incarceration was not fair, but at least he was in a nicer place. I did not cry that day. I felt good and went inside the bunkhouse to see what it looked like. It was a plain, spacious room with many bunk beds. Everything was neat, almost military style. I could see that the food was better because the inmates didn't look as starved. They wore dark, blue denim-like uniforms consisting of pants and shirts with long sleeves. Dad was certainly in a better place, but it was still difficult. I could feel the doom and injustice in my bones.

Walking back from the farm to the bus depot, my sister was crying. At the farm she had met one of the countless thousands of Cuban souls with a story to tell about the horrible effects of a stolen revolution and a lost republic. It was a story of how, for the sake of freedom, people took desperate actions that led to terrible human loss. It was another story of betrayal by our own.

Fidel tried to reduce the number of families fleeing Cuba by prohibiting young men of military age—eighteen to twenty-seven—from leaving the country on the Freedom Flights. As a result, families were broken up or, in many cases, were trapped in Cuba because they did not want to abandon their male youth. The result was that in an effort to stay together and live in freedom, many families tried to escape illegally by sea.

The prisoner my sister had talked to was married to a beautiful swim champion from a time in Cuba when champions were not government trophies. The man was of military age and was one of those not eligible for the Freedom Flights, so he and his wife decided to escape Cuba in a small boat. Other family members wanted to join them. They could not say no to their family members, so the small boat was overloaded. *After all, it was only ninety miles*, they thought. This ninety-mile story has played out over and over again with the same outcome. In the beginning, luck seemed to be on their side; they managed to leave land undetected. They were in high seas when the weather and their luck changed. In the storm that broke out, they were nothing more than a speck in the turbulent ocean. The small boat capsized, and they were all thrown into the water. Those who could swim tried their best to save themselves. The prisoner watched as the ocean swallowed every member of his family. Except for him, they all perished, including his wife.

Somehow, the ocean that took everything away from him brought him back to shore. He didn't know how long he lay on the deserted beach. When he came to, he started looking for survivors and for a fellow Cuban to help him. He found a man who lived nearby. He poured out his suffering and aching soul to this man. The man told him to stay where he was while he went for help. When he returned, he brought the militia and turned in his countryman for trying to leave the country illegally.

People lose compassion when they are brainwashed, intoxicated with power, or truly believe in an evil doctrine, such as communism, that has no concern for the individual.

"I lost my entire family," he told my sister.

All of the prisoners had a story directly connected to Fidel's betrayal. I am sure the rest of the prisoners knew this man's story, but he needed to tell it again. He needed someone on the outside to hear it, probably in the hope that somehow, someday, it would be told to people who would care. It has made its way into this book and to you, the reader. Please spend a moment in sympathy for this man and for all those who were claimed by those "ninety miles" of sea between Cuba and Florida in their desperate bids for freedom.

After our visits, as we walked through the town to the bus, people would look at us from behind their iron-grilled veranda windows. I knew they all knew we were coming back from the prison farm. I could feel their stares. Some watched us out of curiosity; others were neighborhood spies. I am sure our entire trip was carefully observed and monitored by the system and with the help of some of our own people. This was the life and times of Cuba, a formerly friendly and neighborly place.

One afternoon after a visit, I was hot, hungry, and unbearably thirsty. The early afternoon sun was beating down on us without mercy. We finally got to the bus depot and found a taxi, now government owned, headed for Holguín. It was like a minivan with a very low roof. We were squeezed in the back like sardines.

Cubans always referred to the country's out-of-nowhere rainstorms as *la tempestad*. These tempests were always preceded by an impatient roaring, followed by fast-moving, black clouds that dropped heavy rain. On this day, it rained all the way home, from afternoon into night. The lightning was so close that I was sure it was striking the roof of the van. I remember the one working windshield wiper going back and forth, back and forth. Visibility was zero. My mom kept telling me over and over to pray for our safety.

After serving a few months, my father was given passes to visit us. I remember the first time he came home. My mother had managed to get fabric and she had some old, colored thread, so she was able to have a dress made for me. (The time would come in Cuba when one could not find a needle, a safety pin, a zipper, or a button.) My father stood outside our front door. Little by little, a small crowd began to form in front of our house as neighbors came over to welcome him back. It was about time for school to let out, and Marta, my noncommunist schoolmate, stopped by on her way home to show her support. Everyone who saw my father outside that day made a point of coming to say hello, for they knew how unfair his incarceration was.

A few months later, the government transferred my father to conditional house arrest and he finished his one-year sentence at home. The regime had put all of us through hell, and my father's early release from prison did not signal the end of the government's plaguing us. For now, though, we were all right and all together again.

Fifteen

Nature's Respite

Indoctrination in school—including instillation of hatred for the United States—continued to be part of the daily curriculum and was drilled into the young Cuban mind. Every day in school, we had to write the designated year on top of our notebook paper. The communist mouthpiece we had for a teacher would remind us every morning, "First write the date, and under the date on the next line write, 'Año del Vietnam Heroico.'"

The year's slogan was tied to Fidel's having established ties with North Vietnam in 1966. In school, our new hero was Ho Chi Minh. It was Ho Chi Minh this and Ho Chi Minh that. Not only did we have to see Lenin, Guevara, and our apostle Martí together on billboards, but now we also had to see Ho Chi Minh next to Martí.

I didn't know much about North Vietnam, but one day we went to our friend Fe's house on Calle Martí, right next to the river. She told my mother that a friend of hers who left Cuba to save her family from communism had lost both her sons fighting in Vietnam. *Oh, my God*, I remember thinking.

The year 1967 did hold a sliver of justice for Cubans. Ernesto Che Guevara was killed in Bolivia on October 8th. The foreigner who had held a gun and executed so many good, brilliant, and innocent Cubans at La Cabaña was captured by the Bolivian army and killed.

Let the world think whatever they will. Cubans have always known Guevara's death could be attributed to Fidel. We know Fidel. Does anyone honestly think Fidel was going to share the stage with Guevara? After making Guevara president of Cuba's National Bank and sending him all over the world as an unofficial ambassador, Fidel sent Guevara to Bolivia and cut off backup and supplies.[39] That sounds like a demotion to me; maybe even a setup.

As time went on, people became more innovative in their attempts to escape Cuba, but the government made it harder and harder to get out. Stories of Cubans taking chances to escape to freedom continued to seep into our home almost daily.

My mom came home with news of one of the latest, most poignant tragedies. A family in Guantánamo had access to a good-sized truck. The entire large family, couples with children, grandparents, aunts, and uncles—all generations and branches of the same family—got in the truck. There were about fifty people in all. The plan was to speed directly into the fence that separated Cuban territory from U.S. territory, go over the smashed fence in the truck, and ask for asylum on the American side. The plan was brilliant, and it worked until the truck began to speed toward the fence and an Eastern Bloc guard on the Cuban side realized what they were going to do. He shot the driver, and the truck crashed near the fence. The rest was madness. Realizing what had happened, the family streamed out of the truck, trying to get to the American side. The guards opened fire. Some of the family members made it to liberty; many didn't. The ones who didn't died only a few steps from freedom.

Any American service person stationed at the U.S. base at Guantánamo during the 1960s and early 1970s will tell you that all they heard at night was automatic machine-gun fire. The border militiamen were not practicing. They were gunning down Cubans who were trying to escape. Finally, in order to deter Cubans from trying to reach the Guantánamo base, Fidel layered the Cuban side of the fence with land mines.

Another story that especially touched my heart was of a woman who, like the man my sister met at the prison work farm, was the only survivor of yet another small boat attempt at freedom. After her party became lost at sea, the winds turned and capsized their boat. She saw her only daughter drown along with the rest of her family. Somehow, she managed to cling to a piece of wood. The coast militia rescued her and brought her, hysterical with grief, to the police station. I remember the anguish I felt for this woman and her pain. And the stories just kept coming, every day, endlessly.

My grandmother's house, like many other houses in Cuba, had a deep lot with a *traspatio*, which was a backyard garden behind an enclosed, rear patio garden. The *traspatio* was usually left to nature, although some people had fruit trees and chicken coops. At times, to get away from it all, I would go to my grandmother's house and hide in my secret garden, her *traspatio*. There I would spend hours among the rose bushes and the majestic coconut trees. There was a hose hole in the patio wall by the *lavadero*,* so the rose bushes could be watered. When the government did not shut the water off, I would water the rose bushes with my grandmother's worn-out pink hose. Sometimes after I had watered for a long time, she would come and shut off the water. I just wanted to stay there watering those rose bushes forever. I would also rake and observe nature. Sometimes I would rake till the ground was smooth and clean of all debris and then come back the next morning to see paw prints made by all of the nocturnal creatures. Somehow I managed to plant a pumpkin seed and could not believe the size of the pumpkin I grew. I could easily sit on it without bruising it. I also planted lettuce and watched it grow.

Looking back, I realize that the human mind needs a place to go to get away. It needs a hobby to work at that is something we do just because we want to, not because we have to. We need something or someplace that brings us joy or inner peace, or both. Having lived the first twelve years of my life under communist tyranny and forty-two years in freedom, I understand why so many people put their lives at risk to regain their freedom and to live in liberty with a place to rest. Most

---

* A sink used for washing clothes, made out of cement and attached to plumbing with running water.

Americans have no idea—no idea—of the freedoms and the liberty they have and take for granted.

Not all of the stories of escape attempts ended in tragedy. For example, in 2002, the *Free Republic* reported on how a Cuban man hid in the wheel compartment of a DC-10 jet headed for Canada from Cuba. Temperatures at thirty thousand feet are nearly forty degrees below zero. Somehow, this man wrapped his shirt around heating pipes under the plane and clung on for four hours before landing in Canada, unhurt.

Ask yourself: how bad would your life have to be before you attempted such a dangerous and nearly hopeless escape? That is how bad life under Fidel Castro was and is.

Only on Sundays and Just for a Little While

Like everything else, television stations became state run. With the exception of Soviet Eastern Bloc movies, no new movies came into Cuba. We had an old black-and-white television. It was a big, square box that sat on a black, metal four-legged table. I think it was a Philco. Little by little, communist propaganda infiltrated every show. There were no commercials; advertising was eliminated, for there are no goods to advertise in a communist society. Old American cartoons and movies were shown, along with old Latin American movies. We used to cross our fingers that they would not be repeats we had seen many times over, but they usually were.

One night when we turned on the television, we just got white snow. Each evening was the same until, come Sunday, all of a sudden the white snow went away and we could see the television clearly for two hours. Then white snow came on again. My father took the television to a barely functioning electrics shop. The repair people told him nothing was wrong with the television.

We finally figured out the "snow" was caused by the government. They were so mean and spiteful that they were rationing pleasure by blocking the signal periodically during the week. Two of our neighbors worked at the electrics shop. Looking back, I am sure they knew what the government was doing, but no one ever said anything for fear their words would be construed as criticizing the government. After a while, the signal was totally blocked.

Our Parish, San Isidoro

San Isidoro, my family's parish, was and is one of Holguín's two mission-style Catholic churches. It rivaled San José, Holguín's other mission-style church, until after Vatican II. Father Peña went crazy and tore all of the interior wall plaster apart in an effort to remove the elaborate architecture and all of the saints' statues in a misinterpretation of Vatican II documents. He could not know that due to the thousands of parishioners who would die, disappear, or flee Cuba and the destruction of its economy, he would not have access to the craftsmanship or materials to repair the walls. Consequently, for as long as I could remember, the inside of our church was torn down to its very bones, the bricks.

A statue of Santa Teresa de Ávila ended up in the house of my sister's friend, who, because her name was Teresa, received it from Father Peña. Teresita's house was a modern, two-story structure on Calle Frexes. The house was a duplex that accommodated two separate families. Teresita lived on the second floor.

I loved going there. The house had a garden portal with trees that kept the area cool and inviting. To the right was the stairway to Teresita's house, which hosted a huge balcony. The interior of the house was super modern. The stylish furniture was upholstered, not made all out of wood like ours, and they had a piano! In the dining room there was a hidden stairway that went down to the first floor. I loved this house! I remember the thrill I felt as a child going up that narrow secret stairway. It was like something out of a movie.

I had an unforgettable experience the day that I saw the statue of Saint Teresa in the back bedroom of Teresita's house. Fidel's laws prohibited religious practice outside of a church building, so the statue was hidden in a corner behind an armoire. You could only see it if you stood right in front of it. I had heard about Catholic schools and nuns, but they were long gone. Father Peña had stripped the church, so Santa Teresa de Ávila was the first nun I had ever seen, even in statue form.

When I saw that statue, I remember experiencing an intense resentment, sadness, and sense of injustice that everything Catholic, everything Christian, had to be practiced in hiding. I felt how unfair it was to force a person to hide a symbol of faith. That day I understood yet another way in which our government system was wrong.

After standing silently before the statue, I left the room and walked to the terrace in the back of the house. It was a good-sized terrace with a tiled, terracotta floor. I reached the edge of the wall and looked down at the tiled, Spanish-style patios beneath me. Then a driving yet soft wind came over me and engulfed me. The wind was tunnellike, and I could feel it making contact with every part of my skinny body. I could feel it on me and around me in the form of a gentle but strong current that wanted me to notice it. It was cool, refreshing, and warm at the same time. It was fast despite its gentleness, and it was headed somewhere behind me. I got the sense that only I could feel it. It made a different kind of noise from any I had ever heard before.

I remember standing there, letting that sweet wind caress me. I have never felt or experienced anything like it since, and I have never forgotten it. Perhaps it was a sign to me that the government could force us to hide our faith, but it could not separate us from God—we were not hidden from Him.

Church Yes, Freedom No

Freedom of religion and freedom to worship are two very different things. Little did my mother know when I was born and baptized that in as few as four years, freedom of religion would change to "freedom to worship," a ploy to fool the world into believing that the Cuban people could practice their faith.

After Fidel declared himself a Marxist, the practice of religion, whether Catholic, Protestant, or Jewish, was forbidden everywhere except inside a church or temple. The time came in Cuba that when you sneezed, others would not reply, "Jesus," which was the custom.

The new system allowed churches to remain open and priests to remain in their churches, but Fidel tried very hard to destroy the church. A few diehards who had entered a seminary before 1962 were ordained, but in the twelve years I attended San Isidoro, Father Peña was the only priest I ever saw. Soon Father Peña was celebrating mass solo at the altar, because the servers had generally stopped coming. Those who had not left the country were afraid to assist with mass or were in *el servicio militar.*[*] I thought the one altar server who arrived late but came after all was very brave.

Over time, the Roman Catholic Church—its catechism and sacraments, and even church attendance—were reduced to near extinction. If you attended church, you were barred from getting a university education. To further discourage church attendance in Holguín and to mock and kill off the church, the government installed huge loud speakers from electrical poles across from San Isidoro. During mass they would blast loud music and communist propaganda. It was so loud that you could hardly hear Father Peña speak. One day, he commented that the speakers were there to discourage people from going to church. The loudspeakers and various scare tactics worked, for only the brave dared to attend.

Intimidation was another government tactic. One day, my sister and I were sitting in church. All of a sudden, a *miliciano* walked in as if he owned the placed. He headed toward the chapel on the right and walked out that chapel's door. By this time, the military uniform was considered by all Christian

---

[*] Military service.

people—Catholics and Protestants alike—to be evil. My sister and I looked at each other. (Life had become a series of stares, looks, and signals.) We did not recognize the *miliciano*; he wasn't a regular. The government had sent him, I was sure. The fact that he walked in one door and out the other without taking off his cap, without making the sign of the cross, and without kneeling in the chapel told me that.

Since we were leaving the country, the government knew there was no sense in intimidating us about our church attendance, but that didn't mean they didn't try. One day, my sister and I were coming back from church, walking on Calle Martí toward Fomento. All of a sudden, two young men walked up behind us, very close to our heels. We finally had to step aside, and they moved on. Such useful government idiots! It was obvious to me that they were sent by the system to intimidate us, perhaps in exchange for a few extra ounces of beans or rice in their rations. Youth can be so easily misguided, and Cuban youth were very thirsty and anxious to be part of something in a society from which recreation, hobbies, free association, and every small source of joy had been stolen. For many youth, there was nothing to look forward to in life but a few extra favors from the government, even at the cost of mistreating fellow Cubans for no reason.

There was also continuous propaganda. I remember going with my sister to Teatro Infante, the main theater in the center of the city, to see a post-Fidel, Cuban-made movie. Not too long after the film started, my sister pointed out to me that it was a propaganda film degrading the Catholic Church and making fun of priests. No, it was not necessary for the government to close the churches. They had other ways of emptying the pews.

The foremost way the government had of preventing young men from entering the priesthood was mandatory military service beginning at age eighteen. As soon as young men turned eighteen, they were taken away and trained to be *jóvenes comunistas.*[*] Church and God were out of the question for these young men, as we parishioners were about to find out.

One day, San Isidoro's bells started ringing, and they continued to ring on and on. Word got out that a Catholic young man, whose surname was Miranda, had been shot during military exercises on the previous Sunday. The government declared the young martyr's death was a military accident, but actually he was killed for defying the system. When it was time to go to church, he tried to leave training to attend mass. As an example, was executed in front of his peers. Someone learned the truth from good men who had witnessed his execution, and the person ran up to the bell tower and began pulling the bell rope. It seemed to me that the bells were crying out, "We know the truth, and God knows the truth."

This is how the government instilled fear in people. This is how the pews got emptier and emptier and how the young became children of the state and state-bred atheists. Soon church parishioners consisted of older people, sick people, women who had never been married, and those of us who were leaving the country—a small congregation of people who, in the eyes of the government, were no threat.

I still remember Father Peña's homily when he told the congregation not to stop coming to church and not to allow

---

[*] Communist youth.

themselves to be discouraged or intimidated. He was right; it was up to the people not to give up Christianity. Having said that, it was easier said than done. Man's instinct is to survive. There are very few heroes and martyrs in this world.

For centuries, the church doors had remained open during the day for those who wanted to spend quiet time in prayer and adoration. The priest was always around in case he was needed. That was the culture. One day, I noticed that San Isidoro's doors were closed during the daytime. My sister told me that someone had gone in and stolen an item. For decades, no one had ever stolen anything from the church. That would be sacrilegious, and the lowest human being would shy away from such an action. Even the humble and the poor did not steal from the church. As the same thing happened at San José on the other side of town, there was no doubt in my mind that it was a government act to force the churches to close their doors during nonmass hours.

What was stolen? The altar microphones. Fidel's message to the parish priests was clear—you will not be heard.

Sadly, as the communist regime shrank food supplies, the church could no longer continue its long history of helping the poor. Father Peña had to live on the same rations as everyone else. He was as hungry as the rest of us.

Back then I asked myself why Father Peña never fought the system. Why didn't he demand that the government take the outside speakers down? Why didn't he confront the government about the theft that he surely suspected was a government act? The answer is that he would have disappeared like so many others. Instead he resisted in his own way—by continuing to stay in Cuba and say mass every day.

Meet Me in the Bell Tower

Before fear of retaliation from the government grew, children of all races and economic strata would stay after mass for their religious studies, which would be conducted in the pews with the church doors open. I was one of those children.

In the beginning, we had several teachers. You could tell they were learned instructors who had child-motivation skills. I remember receiving blue ribbons and simple, pretty, motivational religious items made of colored construction paper. Eventually supplies disappeared from the market, and there was nothing to give. I wish I had kept those mementos and brought them to the States with me. They meant a lot.

One day, a boy started to write "Año de..." (the communist slogan for the year) on the top of a page in his catechism notebook. Quickly, his mother, who was a refined black parishioner, erased what he wrote and told him that it did not apply to church. Right there a mother made sure her son understood that the indoctrination he received in school was not of Christ. It took only a few seconds, but that mother did a great thing. I was proud of her.

By the time I was close to making my First Communion, we took our religious studies while hidden in the bell tower, where Father Peña kept a chicken. After mass, some of us kids (the number kept getting smaller) would climb up the steep, narrow, rail-less stairway. I remember the scared feeling I had going up those stairs. I always felt as if I were going to fall.

My religious instructor in the bell tower was a beautiful *señorita*. Back then there were still *gente fina*,* and she was very

---

* Refined people.

refined. She had lovely, long, brown hair and creamy skin. Her hands were feminine—soft and delicate with perfectly filed, unpolished nails. She wore lovely, simple bracelets. I admired her. I have never forgotten that young lady who, in hiding, taught us about Christ. She was so beautiful, delicate, and brave. All of those who prepared us for our First Communion, including Father Peña, were very courageous.

One day after mass, I went up the steep stairs. All the way up I went, trying not to look down. When I arrived at the top, another teacher was there.

"Where is Teacher?" I asked her.

"*Se fué*,"* she answered.

The new teacher was sitting there staring into the distance, her notebook pressed against her chest under her crossed arms. Her demeanor seemed to say, "This is what it has come to." She was looking up beyond the bell tower windows. She seemed to be lost in prayer. At the same time, her face wore a look of incredulity, as if not believing what was going on. She had to hide in a church bell tower to teach children, if any came, about Jesus.

I looked at her for a few seconds, and then the meaning of what she said dawned on me. The other teacher had left for the United States on a Freedom Flight. She had received *la salida*,[†] *el telegrama*.[‡] I remember feeling such sadness that she was gone. I wish I had had the wisdom to keep a daily journal of all of the

* She left.
† Permission to leave [Cuba]; "exit, departure."
‡ Telegram.

people I knew, how I knew them, and the dates they left, as well as a record of all of the events, like Anne Frank did, but that was not really encouraged in our schools. Communist regimes are very good at keeping track of people and monitoring their activities, but it is not something they encourage the general population to do.

My teacher's departure was actually typical of the time. Distinguished people were disappearing. Some left the country. Deprivation and persecution stripped those who stayed of all class and dignity. Yet I think it is important for society to have distinguished, honest, successful, well-to-do citizens. They serve as role models for those who wish to better themselves. The success of some keeps the hope of others alive.

I kept going to the bell tower for my secret First Communion preparation and gladly sat on wooden cartons. I was not bothered by the dusty, dirty surroundings, but it did bother me that we had to meet secretly. It reinforced my understanding of Fidel's government. I was too young to realize that Jesus was sitting next to me in that bell tower and was blessing me in more ways than one. At that young age, my Christian values were being shaped—I was learning to do good rather than evil, practice truth rather than deceit, and do right rather than wrong. Yet there in the bell tower, God was blessing me with something else: common sense. I was gaining in discernment. He gave me eyes to see, ears to listen, and the ability to know the truth in the midst of deception, much like the child in *The Emperor's New Clothes* who sees that the emperor is naked.

Years later in the United States, that common sense and gut instinct told me something was very wrong with the direction of some individuals in my church. It seemed to me that these often well-meaning individuals were supporting political movements, the consequences of which they did not understand. The communist-backed rebels wanted to bring in a government like Cuba's, a government worse than the regime my Latin American brothers and sisters were living under at the time. The resulting peace these individuals in my church wanted for my brothers and sisters in Central America would be a false peace that would eventually steal all of the life, including the spiritual life, away from their country. I lived that false peace in Cuba.

Nonetheless, you could have knocked me over with a feather when, fifteen years later, an American nun cornered me at work the minute I told her I was from Cuba. She poured out to me her anti-American, pro-Sandinista communist propaganda. If someone had told me while I sat in the dusty bell tower, with everyone risking so much for our faith, that a nun would fail to radiate the love and peace of Jesus and instead radiate hatred and anger, acting and sounding like the communist mouthpieces in Cuba, I would not have believed that person. What about those precious, priceless *señoritas* who had been willing to put their necks on the line to teach me about Jesus's love and redemption? They had risked more for our shared faith than this nun had. Who was she to say that Fidel's way was right? Historically, the church has honored those who risked much for their faith.

This nun went so far as to point her finger at me and say, "I am sure you disagree since you are from Cuba." Why did being from Cuba disqualify my experience of what communism did to our shared faith? She should have listened and wanted to know what life was really like for Catholics and all people of faith under Fidel.

During the same period, my mother had similar experiences. Many American laypeople were also misinformed about the impact of communism on freedom of religion. One of my own faith asserted, "But you can go to church in Cuba," not giving me a chance to answer. Another tried to trick me into agreement with him by asking questions that insinuated that communism and Christianity were compatible. When I contradicted him based on my own experience, he, like others, justified his position by saying to me, "But you had money." Now what sense did that make? No one, with or without money, was left in peace to practice Christianity or any other faith in communist Cuba.

It still amazes me that even well-educated people, who should know better, are either so infected by ideological propaganda or so misinformed that they have a complete misconception of Cuban society, politics, and economics under the republic and a complete ignorance of the havoc Fidel Castro and Che Guevara wreaked on Cuba.

Some would call my family rich and condemn us for the wealth they imagined we had. Even if we had been wealthy in Cuba, that would not be a sin. I believe God loves a rich person as much as He loves a poor person. As Tevya says in *Fiddler on the Roof,* while there's no shame in being poor, it's no great honor either. Rich or poor has nothing to do with the practice of faith.

I don't believe Jesus wants to persecute and oppress some of God's children to fulfill an ideal of utopian social justice! I believe Jesus wants all people to have a good life on earth. The Christ I met in the bell tower does not tell us to instigate discord among social classes. Instead, if the light of Christ is brought into the souls of both the rich and the poor, amazing things can happen. It is the church that inspires love, compassion, and help, not rigid political ideologies, and certainly not ones that do not recognize the existence of God and unjust peace.

Despite some individuals in our church inflicting so much additional pain on my mother—truly pouring salt on her wounds—we never stopped being Catholic and loving our religion because of the actions of a few. Most clergy stayed on a spiritual path as exemplified by a priest whom I heard give a healing talk. The priest's message focused on the truth that there is no compatibility between communism and Christianity. When I heard this priest's homily, it was as if the same loving God who sat next to me in the bell tower knew my soul needed soothing by hearing truth spoken by members of the clergy.

Finally, I finished my limited religious studies there in the bell tower, and I was ready for my First Communion. There were only a few of us receiving the sacrament because other children who had started their studies with me either had left the country or were being kept away from church by their frightened parents.

My mom wanted me to be dressed in the ways of our religious tradition when making my First Communion. She managed to get simple white fabric to have a white dress made. Sweet Aurora, the matron of our block, who lived directly across from our house, found an old veil I could borrow, but my mother could not find a pair of white shoes—not new, not used, not borrowed. There are people in this world who would say, "Oh well, at least you had a pair of shoes to wear." Well, eventually no shoes would be available of any color.

Turning at the corner of Fomento and Luz Caballero, we heard trumpet music being played by the son of one of the neighborhood spies, who was at her window post. She was a woman of color who had a well-built house before Fidel's rule, a not unusual example of black prosperity in pre-Fidel Cuba, and her son was one of the lucky ones who still had a musical instrument. Actually, it was wonderful to hear music. Life in Fidel's Cuba was so gray; so barren of life; so devoid of color, artistry, and joy. The sound of music was a welcome diversion from the lusterless monotony of life under communism. My mother proudly told the spy that I was making my First Communion and mentioned regretfully that she had not been able to find a pair of white shoes. She so wanted to follow tradition.

Cuba had been a country of traditions: all white for First Holy Communion, no white shoes after September or before May, corduroy for winter, shorts for the beach only, Sunday best when you went shopping in the center of the city, and mourning clothing for a year after the death of a loved one (a tradition that must have been lost with the fabric shortages). There would be no music in the house from the day of the Last Supper on Holy Thursday until the Resurrection on Easter Sunday. We went about our business during Holy Week, but there was reverence. My mother did not believe in going away to have a good time during Easter week; it was a time for quiet reflection.

Fidel robbed Cubans of so many traditions, either directly through persecution and indoctrination or indirectly by removing the wherewithal to practice the traditions. He also created a society such that the people most capable and dedicated to passing on the traditions had no other choice but to flee.

Every Head Turned

When Fidel announced he was a communist, many professionals (including approximately two thousand physicians) left Cuba. Fidel had to stop the hemorrhage, and so after 1962, most professionals, especially physicians, were not allowed to leave the country, even on the Freedom Flights.

One day, word got around Holguín that a physician who lived and had his practice on Calle Aricochea had been arrested along with his family while trying to escape Cuba illegally. *Another horror story*, I thought. *I just don't want to hear another one.* But hear it I did.

Everything went wrong for this family. Somehow the good doctor and his wife, who were about my parents' age, and their very young daughter managed to get away undetected in a small craft. Like thousands before them, they thought, *It's only ninety miles; how hard could it be?* Well, it could be deadly. They, like many others before them, didn't know the ocean. They got lost at sea and, without any shelter from the sun, their little girl almost died of heat stroke. It wasn't clear to me whether they were captured in Cuban waters by the coast guard or they managed to make it back to dry land and were then arrested, but they were caught, arrested, and brought back to their house in Holguín. The doctor escaped imprisonment only because his services were needed.

One Sunday right after their return, my sister and I were sitting in church toward the back, near the door that faces Calle Aricochea. The doctor's wife walked in that entrance with her little girl. She was holding the child's hand and was walking very slowly toward the front of the church with her head up high. Her little girl was wearing a pretty, red dress with white tights and black patent leather shoes that could only have come from family in the States, as you could no longer get anything pretty in Cuba. Every pair of eyes in that church turned to look at them. Every soul in that church bled for them; trapped because the father was a healer in a society for which there was no healing.

A Communist Christmas

Jesus didn't promise us happiness, but he did promise us joy. Fidel's communist system stole all of the joy. Christmas was upon us, and the government banned the traditional use of festive outdoor lights, which signified the joy of *Las Navidades*.[*] People who used to put up a Christmas tree inside their houses were afraid to do so. Everything was gray and dark. All joy, religious or secular, was stolen out of our lives and replaced with monotony.

One day, I went to a neighbor's house. Her aunt had a Christmas tree hidden inside her armoire. I had never seen a Christmas tree, and I thought the Christmas decorations were beautiful. After I came home, I tried to think of a way of having my own Christmas tree. We still had cotton then, so I took an

---

* The Christmas season.

old, dead tree branch and wrapped cotton around the branches. I took the colored aluminum that wrapped a wine cork (this was the last year wine was available in stores) and hung it from the branch together with a couple of Christmas ornaments my nephew's cousin gave me. Then I placed the branch behind the column between the living room and dining room, facing the back so no one could see it from the street. It was a pitiful tree, but a brave one.

The following year, Lent and Easter came, and the government prohibited the traditional outdoor procession behind the cross. Father Peña told us we could not go outside, but we could have our procession inside. We walked behind the cross inside the church with the doors closed. A procession outside the church would have symbolized freedom of religion.

As a survivor of religious persecution, I am acutely aware of every governmental intrusion into the lives of private citizens, most especially when the government of my adoptive country and religious freedoms are involved. I believe in religious freedom with all my soul, for all people of all faiths. It is the beacon of civilization; the beacon of hope for humankind. If it is extinguished, there will only be total darkness; endless night.

You Do What You Have to Until You Can't Do It Anymore

As the saying goes, necessity is the mother of invention; we human beings will do whatever we have to do to survive.

In addition to roses and several coconut trees, my grandmother's *traspatio* had a chicken coop. The coop was an enclosure made of wire and old, tall, wooden sticks with a gate of the same. Until approximately 1966, the chickens stayed there day and night. There was no way to hide them because every day at dawn, the rooster made its presence known.

Yet a chicken coop and a garden only provide food for a family if others are also able to have gardens and chicken coops. Guess what happens when people who live in the city get hungry and they know there are chickens and vegetables in a backyard?

As Castro imposed meager rations with *la libreta*, making it difficult, and in some cases illegal, for anyone to get additional food, the situation in the cities became dire. Hunger got worse by the day, and chickens began to disappear by night. It was decided that my grandmother's chickens had to be brought into the walled patio at night. In the early evening, while it was still daylight, the chickens were guided out of the coop and into the patio. As a child, I marveled at how very soon the chickens were trained to come out of the coop in the evening and into the cemented backyard. The mother hens would settle under the *lavadero*, and their chicks would automatically crawl under their bodies for warmth and safety. I remember standing there and thinking that the motherly cluck of the hens with their cheeping brood was the most soothing, touching, and loving thing I had ever heard.

It was in my grandmother's guest room, with its ordinary bed and faded red bedspread, that I first saw the miracle of life. The room had two doors and a window. One door led to the cemented backyard and the other to the interior of the house. The window looked out to the chicken coop, where I could see that one of the chicks had decided to start hatching.

Poor thing, it was having all kinds of problems. My grandmother picked up the egg, brought it in, and put it on the bed. We sat there, the two of us, and watched the little fellow struggle to come out of its shell. Eventually the little creature, so fragile and vulnerable, pecked his way out. There was a piece of shell stuck to the chick that it couldn't shake it off. My grandmother gently removed the shell. There was sunlight on a corner of the bed, so we put the chick there to warm up. Eventually we returned it to the mother hen. Somehow this led to a question.

"Why is there only one rooster in the chicken coop?"

"There can only be one rooster in the chicken coop," my grandmother answered. "If you have more than one, they will fight until one of them is dead. Roosters won't let the hens have more than one rooster."

"Why have a rooster at all?" I asked.

"Without the rooster, the hens' eggs won't produce chicks," she said. She had knowledge; I had inexperience. It was the old talking to the very young about the miracle of life.

Normally when chickens are raised mostly for eggs, you kill a chicken for meat only when it is at the end of its laying years. Some of the many eggs laid become fertile, and you never run out of chickens. Eventually, however, under Fidel, we had to start killing our laying hens for food, and soon there were no chickens and no eggs.

The Incubator

As times got tougher, people started getting more innovative. My mom learned from an acquaintance how to incubate eggs.

She managed to get a whole bunch of fertile eggs from some-where. My father had a hanging work lamp with a light bulb that still worked. Mom took the eggs and all of the supplies to my grandmother's house, and there in the guestroom—my mother's and my refuge—my mom and grandmother set up the hanging lamp to keep the eggs warm. It worked. In a few weeks we had chicks, but we soon realized that we wouldn't have enough food for them and we couldn't let them loose in the *traspatio* to search for their own food because they would become prey to cats. We tried our best and got some results from the experiment, but then the bulb went out and we still had to keep the chicks warm. We could not buy a light bulb in any store. Light bulbs had become a luxury item. At night we had to walk around with a candle, when we were lucky enough to have a candle, either because a room no longer had a bulb or because the government had cut off the power that night.

My Mother the Surgeon

The few chickens we had left were getting pretty hungry. When we were lucky enough to have stale bread, the chickens would get lucky too. I would wet the bread and feed it to them. Even animals gulp down their food when they are starving.

One day, my mom, my grandmother, and I were talking in the backyard. All of a sudden a chicken spotted what turned out to be a dried-up, dead mouse and gulped it down in a split second. My grandmother and mother intuitively knew that the mouse had most likely died of rat poison. They looked at each other, knowing that if that were the case, the chicken would also die. My mother ran inside and got a pair of scissors, thread, and a needle. While my grandmother held the chicken, my mother cut the skin in front of the chicken's neck, cut into her gullet, pulled out the dried-up mouse (which was still there, whole), sewed up the incision, and released the chicken. I just stood there, speechless, looking at the chicken, which had not struggled or shown any sign of being in pain. The entire procedure did not take more than one minute. After the wound was sewn up, the chicken went about its business as if nothing had happened.

My mother was an awesome woman: resourceful, smart, and brave.

The Mosquito Net

Since Dr. Carlos Finlay, a Cuban physician, had proved that mosquitoes carried malaria, *el mosquitero** had been a Cuban priority. Every Cuban, rich or poor, in the city or out in the country, had a mosquito net.

We always slept with the windows open, even in the winter when a blanket was needed, such was the humidity most of the year. Mosquitoes were free to fly through the house. Before Fidel, some people who had more modern homes had begun to put screens on their windows, but screens kept the air from circulating through the house. Air conditioners, like water heaters, were uncommon conveniences and only for the more well-to-do or the communist elite. We did not have a water heater;

---

* Mosquito net

for bathing in winter we warmed water in a pot. The day would come that if you had an operational rotating table fan, you would be considered rich by your fellow Cubans. Rich is such a relative term.

As in nearly every other Cuban house, a mosquito net hung in every bedroom of our home. The net hung from four nails, one in each corner of the room, or for people who were more well off, from the bedposts of four-poster beds. Every night before going to bed, we took the mosquito net out of the armoire, hung it up by its four strings, and made sure no mosquitoes had gotten beneath it while we were hanging it. Then under it we went. In the morning, the net came off and was bundled back into the armoire. Some people left their nets rolled up and stretched from the two nails over the headboard, but my mom felt that looked trashy. Nothing was stored under our beds either. That looked trashy too. The bed was made, and pajamas were folded and placed under the pillow.

Once I noticed the mosquito net was dusty. I asked my mom why we didn't wash it. She told me we didn't wash mosquito nets because they might fall apart. I understood that "they might fall apart" meant we would not be able to replace them.

The Day the Garbage Truck Stopped Coming

The garbage truck routinely came by once a week. It was a big truck with two men performing the collection. One would throw the garbage can from the sidewalk to the man inside the truck, who emptied it and threw it back to the man on the sidewalk. As Fidel continued destroying the economy and basic goods became impossible to find, a lot of discards were kept. Additionally, there were no canned or packaged goods anymore, so there was no packaging to throw out. People had to bring their own containers for cooking oil and for petroleum, when those items were available. If the bottle broke, there was great anxiety. We ate everything that was edible, and a neighbor begged my mother not to throw away the plantain and yucca skins, which were not very edible, for the pig she was hiding in her backyard.

Then one day, just like the fire truck before it, the garbage truck did not come anymore.

The Water Runs Dry

Cuban people were introduced to intermittent thirst. Faucet water had not yet been treated to be safe drinking water, and it sure wasn't going to happen under Fidel. Drinking water always came from a spring.

In Holguín, the private company that distributed spring water to our neighborhood was El Fraile. There was a designated delivery day for each neighborhood. The deliveryman came in with a big jug full of fresh water and left with the empty jug. Once Fidel's government took over, El Fraile was mismanaged and ruined like everything else. Days and days would go by without delivery of drinking water. We were fortunate that we had the rainwater well my grandfather had built and that it held clean, pure water to drink. Others had to boil tap water, if there was tap water that day and if their stove still worked.

Imagine no drinking water! Imagine the government purposely shutting off the tap water so you couldn't even boil water on a dilapidated stove!

Our whole neighborhood came to get water from our well. My parents never denied anyone who arrived at our door with a bucket. It did not matter whether they were neighbors we had known for decades or communist newcomers who had been given the houses of our friends who had left Cuba for the States. We were brought up that you don't deny water or food to people in need.

There is an art to getting a bucket of water from a well. It's not that easy. The bucket attached to a rope has to be thrown into the well in a very specific way in order for it to come up full of water. Sometimes people would send their young children, who didn't know how to throw the bucket. As I watched them struggle, I could see how hard life was getting even for the very young.

Back then, all of the buckets were metal, and they rusted very easily and leaked. Furthermore, there was no way to get a new one. My parents never said a word when someone left a trail of water through the house. We would just silently dry the tile floor after they left.

Taking a daily shower became a challenge. When the government purposely shut off the water, we had to fill our own leaky bucket and wash ourselves and rinse quickly before the water ran out. We bathed every day, but in the winter we took our baths quickly with water heated on the stove.

We tried everything to stop the leaks in the bucket, but it was useless. Sometimes family and friends who had left for the

States would send a razor blade for my father or a strip of gum inside a letter. After the excitement of getting gum and chewing it to death, we would try to use the gum to stop the leaks in the bath bucket, but in the end it just didn't work. Once something broke in Castro's Cuba, that was the end of it. You did without.

Grayer Than the Day Before

From this point on, I expected every day to be worse than the one before. What an awful outlook for a child to have! Yet it was all too true.

It is no fun to be poor under any circumstances, but I would rather be poor in freedom than poor in tyranny. As bad as the hunger was, the despair was worse. Things were not going to get better; in fact, experience showed they were going to get worse and worse. No matter how hard we tried, we could not improve our lot. At least if you are poor in a society that allows you the possibility of upward mobility, you have something to work for, to aim for. If you are poor and hungry in a Marxist state, you have no hope for a better life. Things are going to slowly, inexorably, march toward the worst.

Another horrific story reached our home that exemplifies this truth. A poor soul went mad from not having enough food and from listening to her children's hungry cries. The despairing mother sprinkled petroleum on herself and used her last match to escape.

Eventually, the basic durable goods people had before Fidel took over disintegrated and gave way to what we Cubans call *la miseria.** Shoes, clothing, even underwear were rationed and hard to get. Parents tried to give their children birthday and sweet fifteen parties, but it became harder and harder. While all this was going on, the Russians and the Eastern Bloc citizens in our country had their special stores where they had the best of everything. Some people used the black market to get shoes, material for clothes, food, and milk, but after my father's experience, we were very careful. We had nothing to do with the people who were running the black market.

Some cried out, "It's the embargo; it's the U.S. embargo's fault." Yet it wasn't. Fidel's actions were and are responsible for Cubans' *miseria* and Cuba's situation in the world, embargo included.

I was malnourished, but I was still growing. I outgrew my shoes, and it came to the point that I didn't have any shoes that fit. My poor mother tried to get me a pair with her rationing coupons. In my innocent mind, I convinced myself that she would come home with a pair of pretty sneakers like I had seen a neighbor wearing.

I will never forget that day. My mom went to every store, but the shelves were empty. I was across the street at Aurora's portal, so that when my mother turned the corner, I was the first person she saw. She was walking so close to the walls of the houses that her shoulder brushed Fermin's house. I could see she wanted to hide, yet I ran to her and asked, "Did you find a pair of shoes?"

"No," she whispered.

---

* Poverty (misery).

It was a powerful moment for both of us. In my mother's heart was the pain of going to the store with hard-earned money to buy a necessary good for her child and coming home empty-handed, unable to provide something as basic as a pair of shoes. In my heart was the pain of disappointment and deprivation.

I never asked for anything again. I knew that if my parents could get something for me, they would; it was not their fault if they couldn't.

As time went by, I realized that those of us who had applied to leave the country had an invisible scarlet letter branded on our foreheads. It was so clear that we were being discriminated against that my mother quit bothering to go to the stores. Nonetheless, when we came across a store that had a visible supply of cheap Russian pigskin shoes, we tried again. A neighbor and her daughter were going to the store, so my mother gave me money and our ration card. According to the rationing system, I, like other Cuban children, was entitled to one pair of shoes every three years (no matter how fast my feet grew). I got so excited when I saw the cheap shoes in the store. I no longer had socks, but I would have shoes that fit. I had been wearing an old, small pair with the laces undone so that they would not hurt my feet too badly.

The neighbor asked the clerk for a pair of shoes my size. He looked directly at her—he never looked at me—and said, "I don't have any shoes that size." All of the sizes were posted, and there were shoes under each sign. I heard the prolonged silence. Then we left and walked around the park. The neighbor decided to go back to the store to try again. She asked the same male clerk for a pair of shoes my size and told him I was entitled to a pair.

"I don't have shoes her size," he repeated in his mouthpiece tone of voice.[*]

The neighbor gave him a long stare.

It was as if this man knew who I was, although I didn't know him. At least, I didn't think I knew him. Was he afraid? Did he know my mom or my dad and dislike them and therefore took it out on me? Was he a Fidelista who hated us "worms," as Fidel had labeled us? Or was he just plain evil? The three of us walked back home in silence. I once again felt a terrible sense of injustice, even if it was only about a pair of cheap Russian shoes.

Not too long after this, I came home to find a pair of new shoes. They were brown with a strap. I don't know how my parents got them. I did not ask. Yes, they were cheap Russian quality and they soon began to fall apart, but they were big enough. These were the shoes I was wearing when I arrived in the United States three years later.

All children in Cuba lacked basic necessities, not just those who, like us, were being discriminated against. In our school, there was a very poor boy who came to school without shoes. One of Fidel's favorite lines when speaking to reporters is, "You don't see a shoeless Cuban child anywhere." That would only hold true if you were blind. This boy had been poor before Fidel's rule and got even poorer with Fidel. He had rotten teeth;

---

[*] If you never lived in Cuba or left Cuba before 1965, you are not familiar with this strange tone of voice and the demeanor that accompanies it. Only those who witnessed the brainwashing can recognize and understand "comrade" tone and mannerisms.

they were full of cavities that were not going to be filled in a system that claimed everyone had health care.

A sweet boy in school named Bernardo must have told his parents about this poor boy. The parents had a spare pair of shoes, and they had some of the natural Cuban compassion and neighborliness left. They gave these precious shoes to Bernardo to take to the poor boy.

Unfortunately, the boy's big, rough, sockless feet would not fit into the shoes. You could hear a pin drop in the room. It was humiliating for him. This should have been done in the office and not in front of everyone; nevertheless, it was a sweet gesture on Bernardo's part and showed that Cubans still cared about one another. I remember feeling so bad for the shoeless boy. I am sure he felt poorer that day than he had ever felt before.

Sometimes even in hours of great shortages and necessity, someone would make you smile. Try as they might, the communists could not completely stamp out our humanity. One day, I was walking to a nearby lot for mandatory physical education. This so-called physical education consisted of calisthenics and running around because there was no equipment for any organized sports, not even balls to shoot through two bare, rusted hoops, the last remnants of what had once been a fine outdoor gymnasium. My sister had an old pair of plain, white sneakers that were too small for me, but I decided to wear them anyway because I had to attend the class and couldn't go barefoot. I managed to get the sneakers on, but I was almost walking on my toes. To say the least, I was walking funny.

The sports lot was at the end of Calle Martí, past Ana and El Chino's grocery store. When I got to the corner, I heard someone calling my name. A female schoolmate of mine, whose name I don't remember, was at the window of her house next to Hotel Tauler's entrance. She was a girl of color with a very bubbly personality. As already mentioned, before Fidel came to power, Cuba had a vibrant middle class of whites, blacks, Chinese, and mixed ethnicities. Neighborhoods were integrated. Everyone got along, and no one thought anything about the racial mix until Fidel came along and began to preach race. I stopped at the corner and waited for my friend. She had been looking out the window, hoping she would see someone she knew who was going to physical education so she wouldn't have to walk alone.

All of a sudden she looked down at my feet, which were outlined against the sides of the tight-fitting canvas shoes, and started laughing.

"I thought you were walking kind of funny." She was trying to imitate with her fingers how my toes looked. She went on and on, but not in a mean way.

Finally, we both started giggling and then laughing out loud. I told her about my shoe situation. We guffawed all the way to the sports lot. Sometimes you have to laugh. More importantly, you have to keep on walking. You have to keep moving forward.

Few shortages were humorous, but there was another funny situation involving shoes. A couple of over-the-counter drugstore products were still available and not subject to *la libreta*. Drugstores still had something along the lines of milk of magnesia. Cubans who still had white shoes began to use the milk of magnesia to whiten their shoes because white shoe polish was no longer available. After a while, though, the inferior communist milk of magnesia came out pink. The whole neighborhood, my mother included, was in an uproar. Cubans were absolutely sure the government had changed the color of the product on purpose so that people could not use it as shoe polish. As a child, I remember thinking it was funny. I kept imagining everyone walking around in pink shoes. It brought a little humor to a life that was becoming progressively gloomier every day.

I was just one child and there were many others worse off than my family. Our countertop two-burner stove still worked, but some people were not so lucky. Others whose stoves had broken began to cook with rationed coal; that is, when matches were available.

Hunger and anxiety were now Cubans' everyday companions. You'd be surprised how long a person can survive without food or even water in the clammy, tropical heat. Yet every day that went by became more hellish, more filled with unnecessary hardship. *La miseria* had arrived in full force. I remember thinking, even at nine years old, *What kind of government would take the basic comforts and necessities from its people and impose misery?*

A threatening government presence was also part of everyday life. One day, bang, bang, bang. Someone was pounding at our door. I was home alone, so I did not open the door. I climbed on the back of our sofa and looked out the upper part of our window. Two *milicianos* saw me and asked me if I knew where a certain male neighbor of military age was. I told them I had not seen him, and they left.

Youth, especially young men, felt trapped. Sometimes males who wanted to escape went into hiding for a while to confuse the authorities or simply to irritate the system. When the government noticed a male of military age had not been seen in a while, the search was on.

Later we found out that Fidel was coming to Holguín to dedicate one of his people's clinics. For security reasons, the militia had to account for every male who was not a party member. A couple of days later, I was standing at our front door when three cars whisked by, almost bumper to bumper. They were moving so fast that, by the time I realized they were passing, they were already at the corner making a left turn. They were late 1950s or very early 1960s models: shiny, clean, and silent. These were no old, noisy clunkers like everyone who still had a car drove. It must have been Fidel.

Sixteen

1968 Year of the Heroic Guerilla Fighter
Año del Guerrillero Heroico

Los Pioneros*

Despite the fact that many believed that he had set up Guevara to be killed, Fidel dedicated 1968 to Che Guevara, whom he referred to as a heroic figure. By this "Year of the Heroic Guerilla Fighter," most students, except for those of us who were leaving the country, were wearing a red-and-white scarf to school. This scarf signified that the wearer was a young communist Pioneer. Thankfully, we who were leaving were not invited into the party. My feelings were not hurt, that's for sure. I did not feel left out at all. I was happy to stand out in the crowd. I remember thinking, *Good riddance; who wants to wear*

---

* Pioneers. Members of a government organization made up mostly of Cuban children who were required to attend progovernment rallies and who were encouraged to inform on friends and family who engaged in "counter-revolutionary" activities or speech.

that evil kerchief around their neck? Many of the children wearing it didn't even know what it meant.

Once in a while, the school director, a tall, thin woman who sported red lipstick and wore a quality, pre-Castro, white linen outfit, came around to check on children who were not yet Pioneers. She would then send the children home during the school day to ask their parents if they could become Pioneers. By now, parents were not fighting the system, even if they wanted to. Of those who wanted to leave Cuba but could not, many decided that if you can't beat them, it is better to join them and pretend you are in. It was safer that way. Some education, even if it was saturated with indoctrination and lies, was better than no education at all, they thought, and the price of saying no meant you did not get to go on in school. So, sooner or later, all of the children came back to school with a "yes" answer—except for Marta and her brother.

Marta and her brother had recently lost their mom and were being raised by their maternal aunt. Their mother, knowing she was dying and knowing she was leaving her children in a totalitarian communist regime, begged her sister never to allow her children to become communist Pioneers. What a great woman their mom was! Their aunt kept her promise and taught her niece and nephew that the government had no business in their private lives.

The principal and the teacher sent Marta and her brother home with the usual note. Not counting those of us who were leaving Cuba, they were probably the last two kids in my school and maybe in all of Holguín who had not become Pioneers.

They returned to school with the message: "My aunt promised my mother on her death bed that she would never allow us to become Pioneers." They told this to the teacher and principal in front of the whole class. The teacher and principal rolled their eyes in disrespect, looked at each other, and did not pursue the issue. The indoctrination of these two young children would have to wait.

Maybe not for long, though. Perhaps sometime after we left, Marta and her brother would have no choice but to become *jóvenes comunistas*, either to get the government off their backs or to be able to continue their education at the high school level. Yet for now at least, they stood their ground and, regardless of what might happen in the future, the regime would never change their hearts, for a loving and truthful mother had protected those hearts with her dying breath.

La Nueva Medicina*

A family member was at Lenin Hospital after having surgery. She developed a wracking cough. The nurses, who were plentiful and well trained prior to the communist takeover of the hospitals, who would have run to her aid and would have provided her with necessary medication, had been replaced with untrained workers who sat in chairs and slept through the night. She kept begging the on-call worker to get her something for her cough. The worker kept telling her to wait because she was sleeping.

---

* The new medicine.

Another family member who was five months pregnant dropped by Lenin Hospital to make sure everything was all right. The animals, as we soon began to call the Russian, Eastern Bloc physicians Fidel brought to Cuba, put her through labor. She was only two centimeters dilated and was not having any contractions. Excellent Cuban physicians from the University of Havana, a top school, were replaced with these cold, heartless, unqualified communist medicine doctors.

When my baby nephew was about three months old, our family came face to face with Fidel's new health-care system. The encounter confirmed the truth of the double standard in this system.

My father, mother, and I decided to go to visit my father's brother. My father's car had broken down and was parked in front of our house, so we walked to the center of town by Calixto García Park to take a bus. Public transportation, like everything else, had deteriorated, and going anywhere was hell. We waited and waited; the bus did not come. Finally, we returned home. It was a miracle that we came back to the house. My infant nephew was running a very high fever. My sister and my mother ran with him to the hospital. Luckily, a Cuban physician was on call and my godfather was the x-ray tech on duty. They finally diagnosed that my nephew had a kidney infection. The doctor turned to my godfather and pointed to a locked cabinet. He told him the antibiotics were locked up. They were reserved for special patients—the elite party members and for the Russians and Eastern Bloc people. The doctor told my godfather that if he wanted to risk taking some of the antibiotics to go ahead; then he walked away. In a split second, my godfather opened the cabinet, took the vials of antibiotics, and gave them to my mom and sister, who left very quickly to make arrangements to have the daily injections administered secretly. Without the antibiotics, my little nephew could have died, as many Cubans have died since then, even from simple tooth infections.

I wish that those journalists who are so quick to believe that Fidel improved medicine in Cuba knew that these were not isolated cases. But then again, things are not always the way they seem. Journalists report what they see, and so many times they and other visitors were taken to a model location set up as propaganda, where they only saw what the Cuban government wanted them to see.

The sheer number of physicians who fled to the United States is evidence of the excellent health care Cubans had before Fidel. If medical care had been for the rich only, as some assert, and if there had not been nearly universal medical care, how exactly would that many doctors and pharmacists have made a living?

It is common for journalists to report that there is a physician on every block in Cuba now. Well, before Fidel there was a physician on almost every block, and they were far better physicians. In 1957, Cuba ranked third in Latin America for the most physicians and dentists per capita. There were 128 physicians and dentists per 100,000 people, which was equal to the Netherlands at the time, and greater than the United Kingdom and the United States.[*]

---

[*] http://ctp.iccas.miami.edu/FACTS_Web/Cuba%20Facts%20Issue%2043%20December.htm

Private doctors had practices in all of Cuba's cities, Holguín included. In most cases, like the consult of our family cardiologist, their practices were located in the front part of their homes. Those pre-Fidel physicians were from top schools, and they had supplies and proper equipment. The University of Havana's School of Medicine was one of the best in the world. The beauty of it was that medical students paid the same tuition as other university students. When they graduated from medical school, they did not have massive medical school debt. On graduation, they were free to practice medicine wherever they chose; many of them went back home to their provinces to practice. Not all physicians stayed in Havana, as so many would like you to believe.

In addition to the many private consultants, every neighborhood had a *casa de socorro*, which was a twenty-four-hour, seven-day-a-week first-aid station with a doctor, a nurse, an aide, and an ambulance. These emergency stations were run by the government and the Red Cross, along with volunteer professionals. All physicians took turns working at these clinics. The poorest person could drop by in an emergency; if he needed additional medical help, he was automatically transferred by ambulance to the nearest hospital. In our neighborhood, *la Cruz Roja,* as we called it, was on Martí Street. Fidel closed all of these first-aid centers and replaced them with filthy, state-run *policlínicos.*†

---

* The Red Cross.

† Castro's medical services clinics.

Before Fidel, there was also a pharmacy on nearly every corner. One pharmacy in each town had to be open twenty-four hours a day, including on weekends. The pharmacies were stocked with medications to fill the prescriptions. All pharmacists held doctorate degrees. Citizens could walk into any pharmacy and ask the pharmacist's advice and walk out with the right product or over-the-counter medication. Go to the house of any current Cuban physician and you will see a sign that reads, "No Medications Available."

The Cuba Transition Project at the Institute for Cuban & Cuban–American Studies at the University of Miami states that when it comes to health care, pre-Castro Cuba was in excellent condition. Citing United Nations' data, the Project states that in 1957, Cuba had the lowest infant mortality rate in all of Latin America and the thirteenth lowest in the world. Cuba outranked many developed countries in this area, including France, Belgium, West Germany, Austria, Italy, and Spain. Life expectancy before Castro was also among the highest in the world.

In 1958, just before Fidel came into power, Cuba had one hospital bed for each 190 of its more than six million inhabitants, which exceeded the one-bed-per-two-hundred goal of developed nations.[40]

A doctoral candidate at the University of Pittsburgh, Kelly Urban, a Cuban Heritage Collection graduate preprospectus fellow, consulted primary sources and records on Cuba's health-care system from 1902 to 1959. Urban noted that, "President Machado was one of the first politicians to devote significant resources to TB." Following up that good beginning,

"Fulgencio Batista launched an extensive national antituberculosis campaign, led by his newly founded Consejo Nacional de Tuberculosis."* Its program was such a success that the main tuberculosis hospital in Cuba, Topes de Collantes, was closed because it was no longer needed.

Every major city, including Holguín, had a well-run public hospital, such as Hospital Calixto García, the hospital where my grandfather died, where humane medicine was practiced for all Cubans, including the indigent. Many had a military hospital to care for servicemen, active and retired, and their families. Many towns also had specialized maternity hospitals, and Havana was home to a cancer hospital, a pediatric hospital, and Hospital Calixto García Universitario, which was a national hospital supported by the University of Havana and free to all. In addition, surgeons were allowed to perform surgeries both in the large hospitals and in their small hospitals (clínicas). The clínicas were open to all on a fee-per-service basis.

In the 1950s, psychiatry was not as advanced as it is throughout the world today, but Mazorra, Havana's psychiatric hospital established in 1857, operated with the intention of curing or at least helping its patients. Yet under the direction of a long-time friend of Fidel and his brother, Raúl Castro, Mazorra was turned into a torture chamber for dissidents, some as young as sixteen years.[41] Psychiatry changed from curing the human mind to molding and destroying the human psyche by attempting to conform it to a political philosophy that denied human nature.

---

* http://library.miami.edu/chc/2013/11/25/scholar-spotlight-kelly-urban/

Imagine a country in which there aren't medications to properly treat the truly mentally ill, but doctors practice abuse of the human mind to brainwash and coerce, and in which electroshock and insulin have become instruments of torture. All this took place inside the walls of a formerly valid hospital. That's Fidel Castro's health care in a nutshell. Everything he did was to perpetuate and strengthen the communist state. Speaking about communism, Russian historian Alexander Solzhenitsyn warned us that communist governments are at war with their own citizens.

More of the Same

As weeks passed, I outgrew my clothes without hope of getting material for new ones. Fortunately, my sister was older, and for a while we were able to alter some of her dresses to fit me. Eventually, though, I just had to wear clothing that was too small. The shoelaces of my "people's" shoes (the ones I was required to wear as part of my school uniform) wore out, and we couldn't find replacements. They also were way too small and hurt my feet. We were all beginning to look like Nikita's wife when she visited the White House during the Kennedy administration: disheveled, communal farm women.

The Cuban people began to look different in other ways too. Before Fidel, poor people had food, even in the cities, if only white rice and garbanzo beans. Now it was impossible to stretch the weekly food rations to last the whole week, and in the cities food was not legally available outside the system. I could now see that hunger was a problem for nearly everyone. With gaunt faces, my fellow Cubans walked slower, their heads tilted to one side. They rarely smiled, and on the street they looked straight ahead in sort of a glazed fashion.

My own hunger pangs hurt more if I breathed in too deeply, so I automatically took short breaths. In school there were many like me—hungry, malnourished, and squeezed into mismatching clothes that didn't fit any more. We were all doing the best we could with what we had. I could tell visually who had access to more food than others. Usually they were the ones with the strongest communist party ties, so it was not a system where a country was only poor and there wasn't enough. As George Orwell noted in *Animal Farm*, a communist society proclaims that all are equal—it's just that some are more equal than others.

School continued to be useless, with Lenin this and Ho Chi Minh that; Yankee imperialism and Americans are evil; Russia is our friend and the United States is our enemy, etc.

At home, my mother told me the truth: "Americans are good, communism is evil. Our heroes of liberty are Martí and Maceo, among others. Camilo Cienfuegos was all goodness; Fidel and Raúl, all evil. Che Guevara was an evil intruder in Cuba, just like the Russians and the Eastern Bloc are the intruders now." There, while doing laundry at the *lavadero*, she would tell me the truth and correct all of the indoctrination they fed us in school. It was there, while she washed clothes by hand, that she would tell me plainly and simply, "In the United States, you don't have to be afraid to go to church. In the United States, you don't have to be afraid to believe in God. In the United States, there is plenty of food and basic needs are met. In the United States, you will live in liberty." There, by the *lavadero*, she taught me to love my soon-to-be-adoptive country, the United States of America.

The Final Takeover

In 1968 Fidel's government announced that all home repairs in Cuba were the responsibility of the government. There were no supplies for the owners to fix their homes anyway, but people had made what efforts they could. Now buildings of all sorts started to decay, waiting for the government to come and repair them, which didn't happen. Toilets backed up for lack of repair and lack of running water. We were lucky that we had the well and had plenty of water to keep the toilet flushed, even if we had to carry it in a leaky bucket. Imagine a whole nation waiting for the government to repair a toilet or a leaking roof.

Although some of the new party elite could get repairs done, in time the number of party elite decreased, and those who were eliminated joined the rest of us in ruin.

The needless decay of every beautiful city in Cuba was underway, but now something much bigger and more painful was coming—*La Ofensiva Revolucionaria,** as Fidel called it. The people called it *La Intervención de los Negocios Propios.*† On March 13, 1968, the takeover of *fifty thousand medium and small Cuban businesses* started. The takeover took place throughout Cuba, even out in the country. It was the death knell of private enterprise.

Fidel had already seized all urban and rural industries. Now he was coming for the mom-and-pop businesses: clothing, housewares, and jewelry stores; photography studios; and restaurants.

---

* The Revolutionary Offense.

† The Takeover of Privately Owned Businesses (by the government without the owners' consent and without recourse or compensation).

Private ownership of every kind of business you could think of was being eliminated. The seizures started from the top down, moving from the biggest businesses to the humblest. If it was privately owned, it was taken over. No one was spared.

As soon as the government seized a business, the word spread rapidly from house to house: "So and so's business was taken away. *Lo intervinierón*,"* I could hear my father and mother whispering about it.

Many business owners knew their day was coming because the bigger, more successful businesses had already met the same fate in 1961 and 1962, and because private clubs and associations, including the Boy Scouts and religious youth organizations, had been shut down. Still, thinking that they might be jailed, these people were afraid to close shop before the takeover reached them, even though they often had little to sell. Others never believed that their little businesses, which they had built with ingenuity, persistence, hard work, and pride, would be taken away. But they were.

The Day They Came for La Quincalla

I will never forget the day in March 1968 when the communist state came to seize our modest family business. As soon as I walked in after school in my gray, communist school uniform, I knew something was wrong. The silence and tension hit me in the face. My father was behind the counter near the back of the business. There were government agents, Cubans, our own

---

* They seized it.

people, taking an inventory. My father's face was gray, like the color of someone who has gone without oxygen for a long time. He was standing there, barely breathing, paralyzed, as if mummified on the spot. No words were necessary. Everything was clear. Fidel's government was taking away everything my parents had worked so hard to build, and there was nothing they could do about it. The atmosphere that day in the hardware store has stuck with me to this day.

How horrific for my parents. My father had already been in jail for no good reason. Now the government was taking his business. My mom ushered me out the door and told me to go to my grandmother's house. *Gray, gray, gray,* I kept thinking as I walked out while the takeover of our store continued. When I left my house that afternoon, I left a private business. When I came back, the business belonged to the state. Just like that, the simple business that had provided a better life, a better standard of living, and a car to go to the beach once in a while was gone.

Communism strips you of all dignity, little by little, until there is nothing left. It will take your livelihood, your body, your soul, and your mind until you have no spirit or any sense of self-responsibility, until you don't know how to take care of yourself, until you are totally dependent on the government for the few scraps it throws at you.

My father had the option of keeping the store open and working for the regime. For about a week after the takeover, he did keep the shop open with a government-appointed clerk at its helm, but it was too demoralizing. He decided that the state could close the business. They came and took all of the remaining inventory, the cash register, and the supplies. They left the counters, which were of inferior quality, but they took all of the solid wood shelves that ran the length of the back walls.

The remaining counters stayed where they were for weeks. My mother never asked my father to move them. For my parents, it was almost like a period of mourning. One day, a relative came to visit. The counters were light, and he dragged them into the *zaguán*.* My father never mentioned his store again, not in Cuba and not in the United States.

A few weeks later, my schoolmate Gloria's family came by to tell us that their family had received *el telegrama* notifying them that their turn had come up for the Freedom Flights. They had come to say good-bye. I was standing outside our door talking to Gloria, whose father also had been jailed. As I looked inside our living room, I saw my father sitting in a rocking chair right on the spot where the counters had been. There he was, sitting in silence, right where his hardware store had been. His back was facing the front door.

I turned around and whispered to Gloria, "You are so lucky you are leaving this hell." Those were strong words for a young girl, but I spoke the truth.

When Cuban Children Walk By

Today in Holguín, remnants of the lost businesses' signs still exist—La Época, the local El Encanto, and carved in stone, El Grito de Yara—a reminder of a different world.

---

* A covered side corridor leading to the back of the house with its own front entrance onto the street.

In Holguín, before the takeover Parque Calixto García* was surrounded by stores, all laid out in a colonial-like outdoor mall that was protected from the sun and rain by a courtyard roof that went all around the plaza and park. There were stores of every kind: clothing stores, shoe stores, book stores, the photographic Studio Sueiro, a stamp collection store, the Teatro Infante, a ballet studio, optometry shops, and pharmacies. The list goes on and on. Getting a pair of glasses became a thing of the past.

Christmas merchandise went on display in early December. I can still feel the thrill of going to see the toys. It was a tradition. In December, all of the stores would decorate their storefronts for Christmas, and the stores that sold toys would display them in their windows in ways that took my breath away.

I still remember the last time that my sister and I went to see the Christmas windows; the thrill of turning the corner, of looking up, and *there they were*, behind Grito de Yara's huge, glass display windows that came all the way to the ground. The toys were not stocked up on shelves but displayed with a special touch that made it all seem magical. It was Holguín, but in my eyes and heart it was like London's storefronts at Christmastime. After the holidays, which ended with *el Día de los Reyes* on January 6th, the Grito de Yara department store donated all of the unsold toys to the Salvation Army to distribute to poor children.

I can still remember holding my mother's hand and walking into many of the establishments around Calixto García Park. I

---

* Calixto García Park.

can still feel that good, childlike feeling when I sat between my mom and dad in the front seat of our car and we rode around town. All gone. All gone. Nearly all of those businesses are alive now only in my memory and in the memories of those who watched with clear eyes the vanishing of their world.

In addition to the businesses around Calixto García Park, Holguín had hundreds of businesses in the neighborhoods and on the outskirts of town. Some business owners were established, comfortable, lower- and middle-class people who worked hard every day to be self-reliant and to make a contribution to meet their customers' needs. Others had just opened their businesses and were still struggling. By the end of 1968, all of these businesses were confiscated and closed or rendered unrecognizable.

It is with the utmost love, respect, and fond remembrance that I tell about *just a few* of the hard-won and painfully lost small family businesses located in Holguín on Fomento, Luz Caballero, Martí, and Cervantes near where we lived.

During business hours, the broad front doors of our house stood open and our hardware store's wares hung from nails in the doorframes for all to see from the street. My father would set out on the sidewalk some goods such as hay bags, which were used to carry groceries and other purchases. People would stop to look at and often buy items from the display. Salesmen also stopped by the store to give their sales pitches. I remember their conversations with my father and seeing the purchase orders.

Sometimes I helped my father behind the counter. He would sit me up behind the cash register, which was one of those old registers with big, round, numbered buttons that you pressed

Parque Calixto García, 1955. From author's collection

down to record the sale. I would ring up the items, and my father would help me make the correct change. There were big rolls of wrapping paper to package purchases, and rolls of gift wrap. I remember my father's skill at wrapping items so quickly and so nicely.

If I was outside when it was time to close up shop for *la siesta*, I would hear my father taking the cooking and serving utensils off the nails to bring them inside. They clanged against each other, calling me home with a sound like a wind chime.

Toward the end, the salesmen stopped coming, and we had little to sell. Some items trickled in from Franco's Spain, which had not severed ties with Cuba. Whenever we received the precious few goods, our store was mobbed with people hoping to get one or two things they needed. Finally, even these items stopped coming. Then the takeover came, and it all became a thing of the past.

Just a few doors down from us, on the corner of Calles Fomento and Martí, was Ana and El Chino's bodega. The biggest bodega on the block, it took up the whole corner and had entrances on both streets. The outside of the store was modest. The construction was wood, and I remember the portal columns that encircled the store were hunter green. My mother bought all of her groceries there. Counters ran all around the inside of the store, and the stockroom in the back was huge. As a small child I was fascinated when I was allowed to go into the back room. There were bags and bags of flour, rice, and beans. There was a big phone on the wall like the phone in *Little House on the Prairie*'s mercantile store and a huge scale you could stand on. There was also a big, black cat always resting on one of the bags. The cat was there to keep mice away.

The owner was a Chinese immigrant whose last name was Sion, but who was affectionately called "El Chino." He had fled communism in China and settled in Holguín, starting from scratch along with many other Chinese immigrant families. He lived long enough to see Cuba turn communist, but blessedly, he died before the takeover of private businesses. I am glad he did not live to see everything he had built taken away from him by the very system he had fled.

His wife, Ana, the daughter of a full-blooded Spaniard, went on managing the store until the takeover. When any store or restaurant got supplies, they were never enough for the public's needs and desires; people would get in line for days, even for more than a week, before the announced delivery date. I remember it was just after the takeover that a few *Bohemias* came in—not enough for all of the people who were standing around the counter with their arms stretched out, screaming for Ana to throw one their way. Ana's face said to me, "So it has come to this: people screaming and begging for a magazine that by now has become another propagandistic tool of indoctrination."

I was one of those screaming. There was one magazine left when Ana glimpsed me. She threw it in my direction, and I caught it. Perhaps she threw it my way because I was a child or because she knew my parents, who were her loyal customers. I could see the pain of injustice on Ana's face the day they took her business away; the pain of having no recourse. I saw this pain over and over again in the faces of many private-enterprise owners. I knew right then and there that Ana would not keep the bodega open under government ownership, just like my father had not. There was no point. Goods were disappearing, and all control over management had been taken over by the government. After Ana stepped out of the business that was no longer hers, the government converted it into some kind of distribution center for fruits that were not available for general purchase. The government did not remodel or upgrade businesses, so eventually the bodega fell into disrepair. It was leveled about ten years ago.

Across the street from the bodega was Ana Maria's pharmacy. Like the bodega, the pharmacy was large and had entrances on two streets. Before Fidel, it was full of over-the-counter medicines and other supplies. By the time I left, the shelves were empty most of the time.

One of my memories of the pharmacy after Fidel took it over was getting in line when the word got around that feminine napkins had arrived. Ana María had left Cuba, and the new pharmacist always looked angry and frustrated. With the takeover and deprivation, a lot of people developed nervous conditions characterized by anger, agitation, anxiety, or depression. The new pharmacist had orders to screen the line for eligibility to buy. If you looked younger than ten, you did not get to buy feminine napkins because the government had caught on that people were bringing in as many members of their family as possible to buy extra sanitary napkins for use as toilet paper. I remember being in line with my mom and having the pharmacist come over to check me out, squinting his eyes, trying to decide if I was of menstruating age. By this time, there was never enough to eat and I was so thin you could count my bones. He apparently decided to let me stay in line to buy what I needed after this humiliating visual inspection. Communism just robs a human being of all dignity. That is its goal—to grind you down and to break your spirit.

The Hotel Tauler (renamed Hotel Turquino after Fidel opened Cuba to tourism) was kitty-corner from El Chino's, across from the pharmacy on one side and across from the Escuela* Calixto García on the other. I have fond memories of eating at the hotel restaurant on occasion with my family. We always put on our Sunday best when we went out to eat. Although it was not fancy, it was probably the first place I had dinner out in a more formal environment.

---

* School.

The hotel's restaurant played a role in the last time we went out to dinner in Cuba. Oh my God! Another rude awakening! At that time, my father still had a car, so it was before our business was taken over. But things were changing fast. We went to El Tenis, which was a private club with a restaurant open to the public. By the time we arrived, they were out of food due to shortages. From there we drove to Las Auras, an alfresco restaurant outside Holguín, only to find the place was closed up. No supplies equaled no business.

We came home, parked the car, and walked over to Hotel Tauler, which we thought was still privately owned by the Tauler family. We sat in the lobby like we always did to wait for a table. The head waiter, who knew us, walked by and said, "I can't seat you." He kept walking, not giving us time to answer or ask any questions. We could see he felt bad about having to tell us that Cubans were not allowed to eat at that restaurant anymore. Then we knew: the restaurant had been taken over by the government and now served only the party elite, the Russians, the Eastern Bloc, and a few Cubans whom the government housed at the hotel while they were working away from their homes.

After going to three restaurants, we got the message: many Cuban restaurants were closed and the few that remained open were no longer accessible to the Cuban people. The half block walk from Hotel Tauler to our house was the most silent walk I had ever walked. No words were needed. We shared a clear understanding that good things for the Cuban people were all but gone. I was old enough to absorb the reality and to understand it for what it was. We entered the house in silence and withdrew to different rooms.

Not far from our house, there were a couple of really great beverage stands. Rafael's *Batidos de Fruta*[*] and a *guaraper-ía*.[†] They were both just *tinbiriches*—holes-in-the-wall. The *guarapería* had just enough room for a sugar-cane grinder and a counter, but it provided a livelihood and was a source of pride for its owner and his family. When you wanted instant energy that would make you fly, you had a *guarapo*, which had to be made to order with very fresh sugar cane. If the cane was not fresh, the *guarapo* would not be foamy enough; if it sat, it lost its foam. When you walked up to the counter and ordered, they took a couple of sugar canes, ran them through the grinder, and presto, there was this sweet, foamy drink. When you drank it, you were set to go.

Rafael's fruit shakes business was a dream come true for him. He had everything he needed to make the best tropical fruit milkshakes in Holguín. He had several mixers, ice, milk, and fruit. I can still see him mixing those fruit shakes and pour-ing them into glasses. You didn't need much to be a successful businessman, and you did not need much to buy a fruit shake. Rafael was a proud man, happy to have his business and a good livelihood. I remember my mom saying how enraged he was when the government confiscated his business. He had been an ardent Fidel supporter and, like most Cubans, he felt betrayed. Right after the takeover, I ordered a *batido* and as Rafael poured it, I could see he was seething with pure rage. He wasn't mad

---

* Fruit shakes.
† A store that sells *guarapos*, a sugar cane drink.

at me; he was mad at the system and he could not conceal his emotions.

That fruit shake he mixed for me was one of the last ones he made, and it was certainly the last time in Cuba I had something creamy and delicious bought with my parents' hard-earned money. Everything was turning from sweet to sour, from creamy to watery.

One day, I was coming back from physical education, and innocence made me stop at the stand. Rafael was gone, but the government decided to keep the business open, if only for a while. In Rafael's place was a female government employee. I had a little money in my pocket, so I ordered a shake. In her indoctrinated, mouthpiece voice, she informed me that there were no fruit shakes, but she had canned grapefruit juice. I bought the grapefruit juice and took a sip. My body automatically rejected it, and reflexively I spat it out. It was the worst thing I had ever tasted. I remember thinking they must have taken the grapefruits to Russia to make this horrible stuff over there. "Made in Russia" meant crap. That's communism for you: the creamy taste and wholesome ingredients of a fruit shake replaced with cheap, undrinkable fluid. It wasn't much later that even that sour swill disappeared and there was nothing to be sold at Rafael's stand.

It was in La Cafetería on Calle Martí, which was next to the pharmacy, that I became committed to maintaining my dignity when faced with the many indignities communism and life had to offer. La Cafetería was a 1950s-style coffee shop with padded, chrome counter stools and, before Fidel, tasty food and coffee. With collectivization, all of the businesses' supplies were confiscated. La Cafetería was no exception. No longer could you stop by for a cup of coffee or a cold drink. I remember thinking, *Why keep it open?* We would walk by and see the clerk with nothing to sell. Oh well, everyone has a job in a communist country, even if you stand there with your hand on your jaw, doing nothing.

Food and all commodities were very scarce by now. Once in a while the government would send meager, inferior Eastern Bloc supplies, which people were often afraid to eat, to businesses such as the La Cafetería. One day, a few boxes of candy arrived at La Cafetería, but not enough for the approximately one hundred people waiting for the delivery. My mom and I, along with everyone else surrounding the counter, screamed, "Over here, over here!" with our arms and hands reaching out to the male clerk. We were begging, screaming for a cheap box of candy that, before Fidel, would have sat on a shelf along with many others and that people would have bought at their leisure. Finally, the last box of candy was given away. We got none.

It is hard to describe the disappointment I felt. This is what Fidel did to every Cuban child, not just to me. There are no words to describe the degradation one feels when you are pushing, shoving, and begging for food, only to get none. That day, at the age of ten or eleven, I decided to hold my head up high with dignity. I would never beg or demean myself again. From that day on, when I walked by La Cafetería, I didn't even look in.

Not long after, when my classmates and I came out of school, it smelled like La Cafetería was frying some kind of sausage, likely the Russian sausage my mom was afraid to eat for fear that it was contaminated, like so much of the food the new government had to offer. All of a sudden, a whole school full of children, hungry after no breakfast or lunch and with no certainty of dinner, invaded La Cafetería. It was the same chaotic, humiliating scene as when they were selling candy. Scenes like these don't happen unless people are starving. I just kept walking home, feeling such pain in my heart for each and every one of those kids. How hungry they must have been. I was hungry too, but I kept walking. Fidel has fooled the world, making them believe that children in Cuba don't go hungry, when hunger is all urban children in Cuba have known since the mid-1960s.

The peddlers—*el limpiabotas, el manisero, and los quioscos*[*]—were the last ones to go. They were the humblest of private businesses. They were also a perfect example of how someone with desire could find a way to make an honest living. Up until Fidel, Cuba's free market economy offered every Cuban that dream.

The *limpiabotas* was a nice, poor, white man who decided to start his business in the mid-1960s before the takeover of private enterprise was fully implemented. With a wooden caddy and his shoeshine supplies, he went from house to house, knocking on doors and telling people he was on their block shining shoes for their neighbors. Shoes had become very scarce, but no matter how little Cubans had, they liked to look nice. Besides, Cubans tried to patronize those who had just started a new business, however humble. So they would bring their shoes to the door to be shined. When the *limpiabotas* was

---

[*] The shoeshine man, the peanut seller, and the kiosks

done polishing, he would move on to another block. When the shoeshine man stopped coming because he had lost his business to the government, I wondered what dreams he had had for his future. Maybe he had dreamed of buying a shoeshine station and renting space downtown, so he could make a better living and not have to carry his equipment around.

The *manisero* was another humble man who decided to make a better life for himself. He turned a big, metal cracker box into a small, portable oven with hot coals on the bottom to keep the salty peanuts nice and warm. The peanuts were rolled up in white paper cones and placed in the can. He went from block to block holding the can by the handle and calling, "*Manisero, manisero.*" Children and adults alike would run to the door, and for pennies they could have a most nutritious and delicious snack. The peanuts smelled wonderful when he opened the can, and I liked seeing all of the cones lined up inside. There was very little overhead for this man; he ran his business right out of his kitchen. The warm weather in Cuba made it easy for a person to make a living with door-to-door peddling. Then one day, he just did not come around anymore. We knew. Dreams were stolen from vendors, and small, simple joys were stolen from their customers.

Some Cubans ran their small businesses from *quioscos*, providing services or various goods. Food kiosks were the most prevalent, and they were especially visible during the carnivals. The kiosks that I remember most were the ones when the Los Caballitos fair came to town, and the watch repair kiosk that was in a rented space on the shaded veranda right outside Ana and El Chino's grocery store. One day, it was simply gone. Not long after, I saw a huge stack of the kiosks all piled up helter-skelter in an empty lot, just thrown there with complete disregard. Remnants of the businesses remained in some of the kiosks, including some small, brightly colored bags that the sellers had used for food and candy. I took a few for my nephew's first birthday in the hopes that we could get some candy to fill them.

The final step in the takeover of private enterprise was accomplished. There was nothing left. Nothing! Not only did the government confiscate everything, it put people in charge who had no idea how to run the businesses. In short order, if the businesses were not closed, they were run into the ground. You would go out with a quarter in your pocket and come home with a quarter in your pocket. There was nothing to spend it on.

Trillando Café*

The regime decided that housewives leaving on the Freedom Flights had to be punished for leaving Cuba. They must be forced to do some kind of mandatory, unpaid work because Fidel thought this would humiliate them. It was one of the many ways the government singled out those who were choosing to leave Cuba, labeling them counter-revolutionaries. The government converted a small house into a center to thresh coffee beans, and all adult women in the area who had applied for exit were notified that they had to thresh coffee beans if they wanted to be allowed to leave.

---

* Threshing coffee.

It was May 1968 and both my mother and my sister were required to report to work every weekday. There were two shifts, one in the morning and one in the afternoon. The government's goal to humiliate backfired. Every woman who had applied to leave the country was more than happy to cooperate. It was a small price to pay for freedom.

I was dying to see what the process was like. I finally convinced my mother to let me go with her one day. The women were working in an ordinary house very close to the grocery store that was loaded with the best food for the Russians and the Eastern Bloc occupiers. The house had been totally emptied of its usual furniture and was furnished with long, wooden tables and folding wooden chairs that the government had taken away from private businesses.

As soon as I walked in with my mom, I could feel tension among the women. You would think that women who were all in the same boat would get along and make the very best out of a bad situation. Nothing could have been further from the truth. It turned out that some chairs were nicer than others, and the women started arguing over the chairs. Some women brought a more comfortable stool from home with the understanding that it was theirs to use.

I went to the front of the house where there were three chairs lined up outside a makeshift office. I took a chair that wasn't falling apart and placed it next to my mom. I figured no one would complain or want the chair, since I took it from the hall. In just a few minutes, one of the government employees came over and quietly told me one of the workers wanted my chair. I told him I had taken the chair from the hall outside the office. He gave a kind smile, and my mom told me to give him the chair. Poor guy, I think he had a difficult job, supervising a bunch of women. I got up and gave him the chair in the spirit of not doing anything that could lead to the government suspending our departure. *Fear of everything, absolute fear of the slightest thing, is the name of the game,* I remember thinking.

My mom started showing me how to separate the bad beans from the good beans in preparation for threshing. First, you took a fistful from the bag. Second, you spread the beans on the table and took out the ones that were not a rich, dark color. As I was sitting there sorting coffee beans, a thought came to me. Were they going to throw away the bad beans? If so, perhaps I could take them home. Surely we could get some coffee out of them, even if it was bad coffee. It would be better than what we had, which was no coffee at all. I kept contemplating this thought over and over. I wanted to ask my mom, but I was sure she would say no. I finally decided that it was not worth taking the risk.

One day, all of the women were told that the center was closing and that they did not have to report anymore. The program was a failure for the regime because it showed that people were willing to do what they had to in order to leave Cuba.

Pasear en Coche

In Cuba, *pasear en coche* meant to go for a pleasure ride in a horse carriage. *Los cocheros** had been part of Cuba's culture

---

* Coachmen.

since colonial times. You could find *coches** all around any main city park and outside any city church, except in Havana, where the high volume of automobile and bus traffic made it impossible.

The carriages were as beautiful as any you see in European and Canadian cities. The carriage itself was open, with a convertible top made from black leather. *El cochero* was a very neat, well-dressed man who took great pride in polishing and taking care of his carriage. The relationship between *el cochero* and his horse was a close one, so the horses were pampered. It was so wonderful to take a coach ride through a beautiful city and its tree-lined *repartos*.† To go on a carriage ride was one of the most relaxing, simple, and inexpensive pleasures Cuba had to offer. It was magical. I used to love the clip-clop of the horse's hooves rhythmically striking the streets. The sound lulled me at night as I tried to fall asleep.

I remember our last carriage ride. It was 1968, and my sister, a friend, and I went to the park. We did not realize that the carriages had become government property. After all, these businesses were just a horse with a nice carriage attached to it. Silly us; had we not yet learned? Each *cochero* and his *coche* were a private enterprise, a business that came to an end with the takeover.

Nothing seemed out of the ordinary. The carriage was drawn up by the park as always, so we went over. We were so

---

* Although an automobile is also called a *coche*, Cubans usually referred to automobiles as *carros*.

† Suburbs.

excited. Our car wasn't running, so we hadn't done anything fun in a long time. When the *cochero* realized we wanted a leisure ride, he got very nervous and looked around apprehensively. I remember seeing the man's nervousness and realizing that, yes, carriage rides had been taken away from us, and the freedom to run his business the way he saw fit had been taken away from the *cochero*. I felt so very sad. He told us that carriages were no longer for pleasure, but to be used only as taxicabs. He then put his job on the line and gave us a pleasure carriage ride, pretending that we had hired the *coche* as a taxi. He even swung by our house on Calle Fomento. That was the last nice thing we were able to do in Cuba.

And Then, Our Car

My father's very first car was a little, beige used car. One day when I was about four years old, on the way to the beach the car overheated and the engine just exploded. Every valve, every screw, every little part came flying out of that engine compartment. We were all sitting by the side of the road. That was the end of that car. I don't remember how we got home.

My father's next car was a 1948 Chevy, also used. We had such good times in that car. In my father's Chevy we went to the beaches of Caletones, Gibara, and Guarda La Vaca; visited Mayarí, Las Tunas, Bayamo, and Banes; and went out to dinner at El Tenis and Las Auras. Other times we would just go cruising. "*Vamos a pasear en carro,*"* my parents would say. Our

---

* Let's go for a drive.

car wasn't just a means of socializing; it was also the business car. The relationship between *los viajantes de comercio** who supplied the businesses and business owners was a close one. It was not unusual for a salesman to extend an invitation to a business owner to bring his family to visit his own family out of town and vice versa. I remember sitting in many modest living rooms in other towns and cities near Holguín while visiting the families of the industrious salesmen.

Maybe a year after my father's release from jail and after the confiscation of his business, the government came for his car. I think that in any society, owning your own car is a sign of success. It is also a symbol of and a very real vehicle for freedom—freedom to go anywhere you want. That is why Fidel's government had to humiliate my father one more time.

Dad's red Chevy was parked across from our house. (Well, it had been red before the sun faded it to a dull pink.) One day, the *milicianos* showed up with a tow truck and simply told my father that the car wasn't his anymore and that they had orders to take it. As they were towing away our family car, my father said, "*Que le vaya bien.*"† He turned around and went back in the house. One more thing he had worked hard for, taken away. He had started with nothing, upgraded to a bicycle, then upgraded again to a motorcycle, and then bought a used car. By the time we left the country in 1970, he was back to a bicycle that was broken and could not be fixed for lack of parts.

---

* Traveling salesmen.
† Fare thee well.

I felt relieved I was not home when they took our car away. I still had hopes that it would be repaired, and I remember staring at the spot where the car used to be and thinking, *Our car, our only outlet, our joy, our freedom taken away. What else can they do to us?* It seemed as if I asked this question every time they took something from us, but there would always be one more thing that Fidel took.

Seventeen

Efforts Thwarted

Nineteen sixty-nine was the year that I discovered the Judas Goat eavesdropping at our neighbor's front door. Despite this disturbing event, and although it is not what Fidel meant by *esfuerzo decisivo*, I largely remember 1969 as the year in which more Cubans made a decisive effort to get out of Cuba. Many died trying.

Not everyone who wanted to avail themselves of the Freedom Flights could do so. Many were trapped in communist Cuba. The most common reason families chose not to exit legally was that they did not want to leave behind their eighteen- to twenty-seven-year-old sons, who were banned from emigrating. There's nothing worse than feeling trapped; thus many resorted to taking the risk of trying to get their families out in any way they thought they could.

Leaving Cuba secretly continued to be difficult and often deadly. Once in a while a lucky few would make it. We would rejoice for them when their stories drifted back to us, but not all of the stories were joyful. In fact, stories about Cubans killed or captured while trying to flee the island continued to reach our house daily. Often we knew these people. "Such and such brothers were caught trying to escape," I would hear my parents whispering.

Government paranoia was high. By the previous year, the totalitarian system was so well implemented that the government knew your every move. This meant that many secret arrangements to leave the island were infiltrated by the government from the beginning. For example, if you lived in Oriente and needed to travel to Havana, you became a sitting duck from the minute you walked into the bus station. An informer in Oriente would contact the secret police, and an undercover agent would be waiting for you in Havana when you got off the bus. The agent might be on the bus with you, without your knowing it. They would track every move you made until the end, when they would arrest you or kill you.

One day, a man I didn't know stopped to say hello to my mother and father. He must have known my parents and needed to talk. He and another man had tried to flee to Miami. They took to the ocean, and the ocean was not forgiving that night. Their little boat capsized. The other man struck his head and was knocked unconscious. My parents' acquaintance swam with one arm and held onto and pulled his friend almost to shore; however, the harder he tried to swim the last little distance, the more the ocean fought him. The man related that he was exhausted, and he couldn't hold onto his friend any longer. I remember him saying, "It was as if the ocean would not let me save my friend. It was as if the ocean wanted him." Finally, he had to let him go. He managed to make it to shore undetected. My parents listened in compassionate silence, the only thing they could offer him.

One of the unhappy stories was about a resident of Calle Martí. He was a very tall, elegant, solidly built man. My sister remembers him as a man you would notice anywhere. He dressed well and wore sunglasses. After arranging to leave the country illegally, this good man took off for Havana with a few pieces of family jewelry that he planned to use to barter for his escape or to sell in the States to have a little starter money in his pocket.

Although the government had taken over most private boats, there were a few small row boats left to private owners, some of whom were government informants. When the man from Calle Martí got to the beach in Havana, where he was to meet his contact and get a boat, the secret police were waiting for him.

After two weeks went by, then four weeks, his family knew he should have been able to get word from Miami to his family in Cuba. Two female relatives, fearing the worst, went to Havana. They went straight to the police station, where they described the relative to the police. Due to the man's height and strong physique, the police immediately knew about whom they were asking. Without reservation or feeling, they told the two relatives to go to Cementerio Colón, a historical cemetery in Havana. They added that they had found and confiscated a few pieces of gold jewelry that he had on him when they had searched his body.

The family ran to the cemetery and talked to the gravedigger, who told them he remembered this man and described him exactly. He remembered their relative because he was so heavy that he had difficulty lifting him on his own. He'd had to get help from a coworker. The undertaker told them the secret police had gunned the man down.

What the undertaker next said to the family is imprinted on my mind. I can still hear my mother's voice when she told me his words, "Ay, *señora*, so many mothers think their sons are in the United States, but they are here. I bury at least three people a day."

This cemetery is now a historical tourist stop.

I didn't want to hear any more stories. As I often did during my last four years in Cuba, I fled to my secret garden behind my grandmother's house.

I have imagined that the last seconds of this Holguinero's life were spent running up and down the shore in the dark looking for his freedom ride—perhaps getting right into a small boat and then realizing he had been found out. In my mind's eye, he starts to run; the coast guard shouts, "*Alto, alto*,"* and starts to shoot. This man is big and strong and he keeps running after being shot. It takes several bullets to bring him down. Did he fall forward? Or did he fall backward, looking up at Cuba's sky for the last time? For forty years I have wondered. Only he, the shooters, and a tearful God know exactly how it happened.

A few days after the horrible story circulated, I remember walking by the man's house and seeing a male relative, perhaps

---

* Halt, halt."

a brother or nephew, standing by the front door. He was tall and thin with blue eyes. When I looked into his eyes, I saw so much pain. He was grieving the loss of his loved one. He was grieving the injustice. I could also see anger in his eyes. Fidel never made a communist out of that young man, I am sure.

This was only one man's story. The same fate found thousands and thousands of nameless Cubans who just wanted to escape tyranny. The world will never know how many never made it.

A Mother's Sorrow

Verena was a year ahead of me in school, and she lived on the same side of Calle Martí as our gunned-down neighbor. Verena was another victim of Fidel's regime. She was an only child, and she and her mother lived with her grandparents and aunts and uncles in a multigenerational household. Mother and daughter were inseparable. I remember that Verena was tall and had very long hair.

A few days before Verena left for mandatory "volunteer" farm work, my mother and I bumped into Verena and her mother on Calle Martí. Their family had known my mother's family for a long time, and they stopped briefly to say *buenas.*[*]

Not long after, word got around that Verena had been taken from the farm fields to Lenin Hospital. She was in grave condition, suffering from a blood infection. A few days later, she died. After a hard day of farm work, she had eaten food

---

[*] Hello ("good" from *buenas tardes*, which means "good afternoon").

contaminated with fertilizer. I wonder if she was even given antibiotics.

My mother did not take me to the wake, which was held at Verena's house. Twenty-four hours later, though, I saw her ride by my house for the last time. The funeral procession came down the street from Martí, turned right onto Calle Fomento, and went past my house. The hearse drove very slowly so that the procession of mourners could follow on foot, as was the custom. The immediate relatives walked right behind the hearse, and other relatives and friends followed.

As the procession moved through the streets, all of the neighbors dropped everything they were doing inside their homes and, as was custom, came to their front doors and stood in respect as the hearse and procession went by. My sister, my mother, and I stood there too.

Verena's procession was very long. First I saw the hearse. Then I saw Verena's mother walking behind the hearse, walking with her only child for the very last time. She had refused the passenger seat, which was now occupied by Verena's uncle. She wasn't screaming; no one held her up. She walked so very slowly, just looking straight ahead at her child, an innocent thirteen-year-old girl sacrificed to a witless political system. My mother and I were filled with compassion for her. What strength that mother had!

I watched the procession all of the way to Calle Luz Caballero, where it turned right toward the cemetery. I went back in the house, sat on a chair, and cried.

The next time we went to the cemetery, I saw that Verena's mother had placed a photograph of Verena in the clear bubble of a grave book on their generational family plot. I had walked by that tomb so many times on my way to our family grave.

A couple of weeks after Verena's death, my mother and I once again were walking on Calle Martí, where we bumped into Verena's mother exactly where we had met before. My mom had me with her; Verena's mom was alone. It was such a solemn moment. No explanations were needed. One mother without her daughter looking at another mother with her daughter. How Verena's mother's heart must have ached at that moment. Yet she was so cordial to my mother.

"*Qué tal,** Blanca?"

"*Qué tal?*" my mom answered.

Barrenderos de Calle†

One day, my father and other male heads of household who were waiting to leave on the Freedom Flights were informed that they were Holguín's new street sweepers. It was just one more way Fidel had come up with to try to embarrass those who were leaving the country. As with other such assignments, the program was mandatory and unpaid. The men quickly agreed; anything to be able to leave. If that's what it took, so be it.

The new sweeping crew decided to store the cleaning cart and brooms in the wide *zaguán* of our house. We were so proud to be able to help out, if only by storing the cart and brooms. Every morning the other two men who were assigned to my

---

* How is it going?

† Street sweepers.

father's team would come over to our house, get the cart out, and wait for my father. Then off they would go joyfully on their cleaning route.

If the system's objective was to humiliate the infidels, the plan backfired on them, just as it had with the women. The three men had a ball sweeping the streets. As the team swept, people would come out of their houses, greet them, and invite them in for breakfast. They shared whatever little they had to eat with the sweeping crew. Some people could still get good food from the black market or illegally from relatives living on small farms, so the street sweepers got some good food and needed the nourishment. People who were not able to leave the country told my father's crew that they would gladly clean the streets so as to be able to leave the hellhole Cuba had become.

My mom, God bless her soul, was such an eloquent speaker—sometimes too eloquent—and she just loved to tell anyone who would listen how miserably the street sweeping campaign had backfired on the government. As far as the government agenda went, it was a complete fiasco. Eventually, when the government officials realized that their plan wasn't working and that they were the ones being humiliated, they came for the cart. Just like that. They didn't even say the mandatory assignment was over. They just sent two *milicianos* and a truck to pick up the cart and brooms.

First Man on the Moon in Whispers

"The Americans landed on the moon! The Americans landed on the moon!" my mom whispered to me excitedly. Anything wonderful that happened in the United States brought jubilation for us, even if in whispers.

Apollo 11 had landed on the moon on July 20, 1969. The news spread in hushed voices from person to person and from house to house. People were afraid that they would get in trouble or be thrown in jail if they showed any excitement about, or even knowledge of, the American accomplishment. The Americans landing on the moon was a big blow for Cuba's communist, Russian-backed regime and a great day of celebration for us noncommunists who were fortunate enough to find out about it. Unfortunately, it was also a sad day for every Cuban child, especially school-age children, who were purposely kept in the dark about this historic scientific achievement.

Not long after the landing, the communist version of the moon landing was published on cheap communist paper in the form of a school textbook. I was at home reading my distorted history book aloud: "When the Americans stepped on the moon, they got the surprise of their lives when they saw the Russian flag signaling that the Russians had landed on the moon before the Americans." All of a sudden, I heard my mother laughing, and I knew I was reading a lie. I was grateful to know the truth, even if it was limited as to details. I realized that most Cuban children would grow up believing this lie, along with so many others.

During the same summer, Ramón Grau San Martín, a former president of the Republic of Cuba, died in Havana. His death was also kept quiet by the government, who did not want the nation to focus on the fact that Cuba had once been a republic.

Although the death of a former constitutionally elected president was not mentioned in Cuban schools, a few months later a national day of mourning was declared in observance of Ho Chi Minh's death.

Eighteen

The Harvest

Fidel declared that 1970 would be the year that Cuba produced ten million tons of sugar cane. Propaganda declaring the ten million ton harvest was spread all over state-controlled radio, newspapers, and schools. We students had to write the year's slogan every day on the top of our notebooks before class started.

Despite the hype, and despite Fidel's throwing all of the country's resources into the effort, the goal was not met. Reality did not impede Fidel, however, who considered himself an expert on everything: agriculture, health care, banking, transportation, the environment, education, and on and on. In his mind, he knew more than the experts in their respective fields. I think he really convinced himself he was improving things; it appeared that he deluded himself into believing this goal would be met. In the end, he blamed the shortfall on lack of teamwork among Cubans, but that was not the cause. Eventually Fidel's agrarian reform, which took land away from knowledgeable sugar-cane farmers to have it worked by the armed forces, children in the mandatory "volunteer" farm program, and foreign "advisors" who knew nothing about sugar cane, destroyed one of the most effective agricultural industries in Latin America and the most profitable and well-run industry in Cuba.

Cuban Students Not Worthy

Since 1968, the presence of Russian and Eastern Bloc advisors has been very evident in our schools. In sixth grade at Calixto García School, I had three Russian classmates. While we Cuban students had to make do without any supplies, the Russian and Eastern Bloc children sitting beside us had it all. While we were wearing patched, ill-fitting clothes, they were nicely dressed. While we had to sharpen our cheap pencils with a used, dangerously dull razor blade because the manual, wall-mounted sharpener was broken, they had colored pencil sharpeners, nice rulers, quality paper notebooks, and erasers. They sat there, well-fed from their special access stores, where they could get all of the food that Cubans couldn't. They sat there with all of the supplies and grins on their faces as they watched us struggle. A few years later, these children would be driven to school in plush, air-conditioned buses, while Cuban children, thirsty and usually hungry, walked in the heat.

Initially, I thought that Russia was a wonderful place because these Russian children seemed to have it all. When I expressed my opinion at home, my mother was quick to correct my impression, telling me of the misery prevalent in Russia and explaining that these Russian children had nice things, including plenty of food and milk, only because they were in Cuba.

Our parents had to put their children to bed hungry, while the Russian occupiers' children had three good meals a day. Our parents had already learned to hate the Russians for the pampered, atheist occupiers they were. As time wore on, we Cuban children learned to strongly dislike the invaders as well.

The newly anointed teachers hammered into us that notebooks and textbooks had to be covered to protect them. They never said that it was because the cheap communist paper they were made from, the equivalent of doodle paper, didn't hold up. We knew, though. Since there were no longer any stationery supplies in Cuban stores, it was impossible to follow the mouthpiece teacher's instructions. One child raised his hand and meekly said to the teacher, "We have no supplies to cover our books and notebooks."

The mouthpiece took a step back and told us, "Use newspaper."

Our family was lucky because we still had cotton that we could use as toilet paper, but I remember thinking that some people were already using the propagandistic newspaper for other purposes. Thinking back, that was precisely what Fidel's newspapers were good for.

While on the subject, the school bathrooms were atrocious. There was no toilet paper, and the bathrooms were a sanitation nightmare. Toilets were backed up due to disrepair and intermittent lack of running water. We tried, at all costs, not to go to the bathroom while in school. In contrast, the special elite schools had clean bathrooms and working water fountains with cold water. To fool the world, special guests and foreign reporters were shown the elite schools, and they erroneously thought that every school in Cuba was like the ones they were shown.

Once in a while someone just had to use the bathrooms. One student opened her notebook and ripped a page from it in front of everyone and left for the restroom. We all watched in silence. We were all in the same boat. There is no dignity under communism.

Another time, a girl really needed to go and raised her hand and asked the new mouthpiece-turned-teacher if she could go to the bathroom. She was denied. She asked again and again, then started begging. The teacher kept saying no. All of a sudden, this girl just couldn't hold it anymore and, sitting in her chair, let go until it ran on the floor. The teacher stood there with an I-can't-believe-this look on her face. These were the qualifications for Fidel's ill-trained teachers: no conscience, no heart, no college degree, no dignity, no humanity, no common sense.

Not a single one of us moved. My heart went out to that young lady. I felt so bad for her, and I remember being furious at the teacher and at the system. If that teacher had done that to me and I had told my mother, my mother would have torn her to shreds. I am sure of it.

One of the three Russians in my math class started to irritate me. He sat to my right in the next aisle. He spoke fluent Spanish. The Russians and the Eastern Bloc people received private Spanish lessons in the evening at the downtown library, so many Russians were totally fluent. I remember admiring their fluency, while strongly disliking them.

The Russian boy, who had socks and wore nice leather sandals, was very arrogant and cold. I don't know how our conversation started, but I mentioned God, even though he was a state-bred atheist.

"How come I don't see him? Where is he?" the cold-as-ice, well-fed occupier asked.

"God does exist; I know he exists," I answered him, loud enough that everyone could hear me.

"Where is he? Why can't I see him?" he asked again.

I did not answer him. I was too young to say, "I walk by faith, not by sight." I was too young to ask him if he didn't believe in electricity or radio waves because he could not see them.

I think I would recognize that Russian today. I still remember the shape of his mouth. He was so very cold for one so young.

One day a Russian girl, whom the Russian atheist boy liked, was talking in class to a couple of Cuban girls. She was trying to be friends. She was probably lonely when she went back to her apartment. Fidel built apartment buildings just for the Russians and Eastern Bloc people, who were warned to stay away from Cubans socially, but the girl was just being her age and talking in class. The teacher asked them to stop talking, and they did.

Just then, the red-lipped, white-linen-clad principal came into our classroom. She was making her rounds and must have heard the teacher ask the girls to stop talking. The principal started lecturing the Russian girl. She told her she knew how disciplined Russian children were in Russian schools, for her husband had visited them. (Only the bigwigs were allowed to leave Cuba to visit Russia and Eastern European countries. When they came back they were not the same people. There they got the same pampered treatment that Russians got in Cuba, while ordinary Russians and Eastern Europeans were living on scraps, just like us ordinary Cubans.) The Russian girl hung her head and said nothing.

Sitting behind the there-is-no-God Russian boy was a recently arrived Russian boy. I could see he was not one of the smart Russians the world brags about. Unlike the other two, he did not speak a word of Spanish and was not good in math. I could see his frustration. He just didn't understand, and I felt bad for him. He was also very messy and kept writing and erasing. He was my age, twelve. He had been uprooted from classes in his own language, probably just when he had learned to cope with his learning difficulties.

One day, we had a math test. He did not understand the math problems. There-is-no-God turned around just to tell him what the word problem was about, without telling him the answer. The teacher immediately told him to turn around. The new Russian kid just slammed his eraser on the paper in frustration. Even though the teacher was a college-educated math teacher from the old school, she didn't come over and try to help the new Russian student understand the math problem. In Fidel's schools, if you were not smart and if you didn't get it the first time, you were out of luck.

Little did I know that three months later I would be in this newly arrived Russian boy's shoes, sitting in an American classroom, clueless as to what the teacher was saying or what was required of me. I knew that sometime I was going to move to the United States, but I didn't realize that I, too, would experience the frustration of being uprooted at the difficult age of twelve, that somehow everything I had learned in school would seem to be traumatically yanked out of my brain, and that I would have to start from square one to relearn and reprogram everything in a new language and culture.

Gymnastics

I was tired of the once-a-week, useless physical education routine in the lot at the end of Calle Martí. The school told us that if we took gymnastics, it would take the place of physical education, so off I went to the gymnasium.

As soon as I got there, I could see the gym was a pre-Castro facility. It was located in the upstairs of a building with beautiful, floor-length balcony windows that faced the park near Iglesia San José. The walls were equipped with climbing bars and all of the things gymnasts use. Sometimes I would get to the gym early and climb all of the way up the bars on the wall or look out the balcony windows.

There was also a piano! I was so excited. I remember thinking, how lucky the piano player is that she is able to play the piano and work in a place where there is music.

I did not have the right attire, for it was impossible to get such things anymore. Only the few who had been taking classes for a long time had gymnastics clothing. If you didn't have certain things before Fidel, you were not going to get them. Those of us who had joined by simply showing up wore our comrade shoes, which we took off, and our street clothes.

In addition to realizing the gymnasium was a pre-Castro establishment, I realized that the owner had either left the country or the gym had been taken away from her, like every other private enterprise. Any real quality gymnastics instruction had been sucked out of that place, but it was better than going to the sports lot.

When someone did not have grace or could not keep time, the teacher would cut them from the class in the communist way, without regard for the person's feelings. At the end of the session, we would form a line and the instructor would point and say right in front of everyone, "You, you, and you, don't come back." There was no asking them to stay after the others left and telling them in a kind way. I used to feel bad when the other girls were treated so poorly and dismissed that way. One girl I knew, who lived near the now government-owned bakery, was having all kinds of trouble. If the instructor said left, she went right. Yet I am sure that the former owner would have been kinder to her and to all who were dismissed, saying gently that perhaps gymnastics was not for them.

I must have had some kind of grace, for the instructors did not eliminate me. Every day I waited to be dismissed by the instructor, but it didn't happen. Then one day I said something stupid. Another girl in the class, Isabel, who lived on Luz Caballero, was also leaving the country. For some reason, maybe to make conversation or to become friendlier with the pianist, I told her that Isabel and I were leaving the country. With a quick twist, the pianist turned around and in the most hateful way told us not to come back. She was a black Fidelista, and I understood what she was trying to tell me: *gusanos* are not welcome. Her actions that day were an example of how hateful people get when they allow themselves to be poisoned by other people's twisted ideologies.

There was another girl at the gymnasium who, I could tell, had been doing gymnastics for a long time, for she had the right gear. I also knew she was leaving Cuba on the Freedom Flights, so I went to her and told her that the pianist had told us not to come back because we were leaving Cuba. The girl immediately told me that she was allowed to come because she had been taking lessons there since she was little. Rather than standing up for justice and defending us, she decided to justify her own special position. I was furious.

I went home, did not speak to anyone, and thought about it long and hard. The next day, I went over to Isabel's house and told her we were going back. She kept telling me, "The piano lady told us not to come back because we are leaving Cuba. I am afraid to go back." She was shaking like a leaf, but I managed to convince her. She trembled all the way from her house to the gymnasium.

As we climbed the steps, Isabel was literately hanging onto me. We got there a few minutes before practice. The piano player was already there. She noticed us. I looked straight at her, sending a silent message that said, "We are here. What are you going to do about it?" She looked back, turned around, and walked away. The fact that she did not get someone to eject us told me her actions were personal and grounded in hatred. She had no authority to say what she did; her job was to play the piano. We Cubans referred to people like the piano player as *empachaos.*[*]

The instructor told us it was time to begin. We joined the lesson, and we finished the lesson. I never went back. I had taught that Fidelista a lesson. I never spoke about it to anyone. My sister kept asking me why I stopped going to gymnastics. One of the instructors whom she knew had told her I was doing a fine job and wanted to know why I stopped coming. My sister kept asking. I did not answer.

Last family picture taken in Cuba winter of 1969 from left to right, my mother, my sister holding my nephew, and me

---

[*] Pejorative colloquial term used by those labeled as *gusanos* when referring to people acting in a brainwashed manner. People with a bad case of Fidel "indigestion/constipation."

Waiting

My parents' humble business was gone; our family's used car was gone. Our simple holidays to the beach were gone for lack of transportation. Caletones, Gibara, and Guarda La Vaca were imprinted on my mind. I guess memories don't leave like people do. I remembered the primitive beach house, the sand, the ocean, the precooked picnic my mom would bring. All gone.

Shortages, hunger, and misery prevailed instead.

My grandmother was hanging onto an old sardine can; my mother was keeping an empty face cream container and a black-and-white photograph of her school friend Diana, who left for the United States and whom she would never see again. Aurora across the street was hanging onto an old, red can of talcum powder called Paris. All of these things were symbols of what had been lost and represented a final clinging to the hope of restoration.

At times, the hunger was unbearable. When my father was able to get a bus, he would go to *el campo* to buy food from the *campesinos*, even though it was illegal and dangerous. We were that desperate.

The barter system had begun. Farmers didn't want money; they couldn't buy anything with it. They wanted china, tablecloths, clothing, bedding, and other household goods in exchange for a chicken or a turkey. The farmer always came out way ahead because his livestock reproduced, providing an ongoing supply of food for his family and "currency" with which to barter. Farmers who lived on a couple of acres were the new rich. As humble as their situations were, they had vegetable gardens, chickens, pigs, and perhaps even cows for milk.

Sometimes farmers would even take money because they felt bad that people were starving in the city. How my father must have had to beg to put food on our table. God only knows how much money he had to pay for a chicken or a turkey.

Eventually my father stopped going to the country because the government started setting up roadblocks to keep food from coming into the cities. Fortunately for us, there was light at the end of the tunnel. Our turn would come to leave Cuba. In the United States we would have enough food.

My mom's mood swings had been worsening. Now, as our departure got closer, I began to notice that her personality and demeanor were changing even more. Her vibrant energy was slipping away. At times, I would find her just sitting, apparently lost in thought. It seemed as if the light had gone out of her life and that a terrible sadness was overtaking her.

Fidel's betrayal was of a whole country; yet, to each Cuban, it felt very personal. My mother was one of the people who had adored Fidel, backed him, and supported him. The same Fidel mocked us with Cienfuego's disappearance, rubbing his betrayal and his deceit in Cuban faces. Then there was the Bay of Pigs fiasco, and finally the U.S.–Russian agreement at the Missiles of October Crisis talks, which my mother had seen as the last opportunity for the United States to liberate Cuba and keep it from becoming a Russian satellite. While others had already grieved Fidel's betrayal and realized it was what it was, my mom didn't start grieving until around 1968, when the truth finally hit her full force. The Americans were not coming. Cuba was doomed. It wasn't just a bad dream or a temporary situation. This was it.

The more time that went by, the more my mother's brain became obsessed with Fidel's betrayal. She was wired that way; it was beyond her control. While others had come to terms with Fidel's evil deeds and carried on as best they could, she could not. Before moving to the States, Aurora, who was in her seventies, realized that my mother was not recovering from the betrayal and the loss of the republic. She told my mother, "Blanca, life goes on." It was good advice, but my mom couldn't take it.

My mother was caught between two equally painful alternatives. If she stayed in Cuba, her daughters would have to live in poverty in a communist regime that was growing progressively more intolerable each day. If she left to save her daughters, she would be separated for good from her beloved family of origin. For her, being separated from her family was like being torn from the shelter of a grove and thrust into a storm.

A great interdependency existed between my mother, my grandmother, and my aunts—it was a dependency of the soul and provided companionship, understanding, and just being there for one another. In a family where depression prevailed and where a suicide permanently had undermined their lives, they needed one another. When my mother walked into my grandmother's house, whether in good times or bad, she was her family's light. She was their joy and their comfort. She was their savior. She was the person who loved them unconditionally and protected them. They called her *hada madrina** every

---

* Fairy godmother.

time she walked through the door, bringing whatever little food she could find to share with them.

It was especially hard for my mother to uproot and completely change her life. She had had a problem with disorientation all her life, but in her forty years she had learned Holguín inside out. Now she would have to leave the house her father built and the city she knew, where she had expected to live out her days and where she expected her children to live out theirs. She would have to move to who knows where.

The community was already full of holes. So many of our block neighbors and friends of generations were gone. Fermin and his family, and Alicia and her family, had already left, followed by Fidelito and Mary. They were followed by Aurora and Generoso and his family. There was no one left on the block who had signed up for the Freedom Flights who had not gone, except us. Mother knew we were next.

My mom was such a good woman. She was very generous, and not just with family. She fed the hungry as long as she could and shared well water to the end, but sometimes she was a little too candid for some people's taste. Her brain was wired in such a way that she always had to say what she was thinking. This was not a problem among her Cuban friends of many years, who understood her and accepted her as she was. Now she would have to start all over again, without her understanding neighbors and friends.

Losing your country and your liberty and being forced to choose between your loved ones and freedom is traumatic in the extreme, and it proved too much for my mother. She was certain that her family would suffer catastrophically if she and

233

my father left Cuba. Thus, she was torn and unhappy about the impending trip.

El Telegrama

Our day came for *el telegrama*. It was April 9, 1970. My mom and sister were doing their chores and taking care of my nephew. I was in school. Our front door was closed. There was a knock, and my mother opened the door. A *miliciano* was standing there with a lower-ranking *miliciano* next to him.

"Don't tell me you have *el telegrama*," she said.

"Yes, I do; your turn has come."

The turmoil, the confusion, the uprooting, the unknown future ahead of us, the painful good-byes were all standing right in front of us.

The uprooting process began immediately. The two *milicianos* began the house inventory. The senior officer took a pillowcase and started opening drawers to see what he could take with him. He was sadly disappointed. Aside from the furniture, there was hardly anything left in the house. Little by little, my mother had removed everything that was not screwed to the walls—bedspreads, linens, vases, the radio, the record player, the records—and had given everything to our family and friends or to my father to use for barter. None of it was of great value.

The *miliciano* in charge opened the armoire and all he saw were a couple pairs of my holey underwear. He tossed them aside with great disdain and disappointment. He took an Oriental ashtray of no particular value and dumped it in the pillowcase. His little sidekick got nothing.

Alerted by my mother, a neighbor came to school to get me. I was in class; a class headed by one of the very few qualified teachers left in my school. I remember someone telling me about this teacher and her lifelong dream to see Niagara Falls. She was not married and lived at home with her parents. She had saved money from her teaching job so that she could go to the United States to see the Falls, and she was able to fulfill her dream before Fidel stole the right of Cuban citizens to travel freely abroad. I am sure she was grateful that she had not postponed her trip. As Cuba turned more and more hellish, at least she had a wonderful memory of freedom and beauty.

I went to the classroom door to see what the neighbor wanted. She told me about *el telegrama*. I turned back, grabbed my books, and walked out. My teacher smiled sweetly. She knew I was leaving for the States.

Two weeks later, I was living an hour and a half from the very same Niagara Falls my teacher loved. I always think of her when I drive by the Falls, and it reminds me not to take them—or freedom—for granted.

As I walked out of the schoolyard toward my house, the enormity of what we were about to do hit me, and I became hysterical and began screaming, "I don't want to go, I don't want to go." Some of my mother's mental and emotional ambivalence must have affected me. Also, we cling to the familiar, no matter how awful it is. All of the built up tensions in me were coming out.

Our neighbor took me to my grandmother's house. The government people were still in our house, and she was afraid that if they heard me, they would revoke our visas. After a while,

I went home and learned that the government had ordered us to vacate our house in one week. That would be April 16, 1970.

Sweet School Friends

When word got around that a student was leaving for the United States, all of the others who were still waiting for *el telegrama* would tell their parents. One of my friend's parents invited me to their home in the original Reparto Peralta, which was named after one of the city's founding families. Although some of Peralta's residents were descendants of Cuba's original, most-prominent Spanish and Cuban citizens, they all worked for a living.

The invitation was a sign of support and solidarity. It was a sweet gesture that will stay with me always. The invitation took me to my favorite place in Holguín. Some of the houses in the suburb were modern. Others were built in the 1800s in Spanish architectural style, with huge iron gates at their entrances and huge glass doors protected by gorgeously designed iron rods. None of these houses can be compared to the mansions of Newport, Rhode Island, to be sure, but looking back, they were my Vanderbilt mansions.

Reparto Peralta was also a garden paradise, and in my eyes there was no place like it. I can only describe it as a Cuban Key West. The *reparto* was cool and refreshing. Its streets were a *florida*,* lined with colorful, tropical, front-yard gardens and flowering trees that seemed to extend an invitation, "Come

---

* A flower-filled place.

walk in my shade that I may offer you natural coolness and relief from *el sol que raja piedras.*"*

Several years before, my parents had been able to get me a pair of roller skates. They were the kind you adjusted and strapped to your shoes. There was a park tucked under the *florida*, and one of its paths was sloped and of what I would now describe as handicap width. A few childhood friends and I would roller skate down that incline over and over again. It was magical; a sense of pure freedom. I loved it.

The visit just before we left was the last time that I saw it all. When their owners immigrated to the United States, not a single one of the upscale houses in El Reparto Peralta went to a poor family or was divided to house several families, as would have been in alignment with Fidel's supposed ideals. All those houses went to the upper echelons of the communist party and to the new Cuban doctors—a new elite.

Before we left our house for the last time, a group of girls from school got together and came by my house to say good-bye. On a different day, one school friend came by herself. She was a short, stocky girl who had been orphaned and who lived with a family on Fomento in a simple house very much like ours. She helped the family with domestic chores in exchange for room and board. She had had a hard life. I remember looking at her hands. Her knuckles and cuticles showed that she did all of the washing for the family. I remember her school uniform being well ironed in a way that only someone who ironed

---

* The sun [so hot] that [it] splits rocks. (A phrase Cubans used to refer to the midday sun from noon to at least 2:00 p.m.)

for a living could accomplish. She had many responsibilities before going to school—and at such a young age in a country where life would only get harder. The one bright spot was that, although she paid for her keep with her work, the family she lived with had come to love her very much.

My friend was my age, and in her twelve years she had already learned what I was about to learn—many good-byes are final. Life had forced her to grow up beyond her years. She knew those of us who were leaving would change and would be caught up in a new life. That was the way it was. She knew by experience that life was not fair. She knew I was leaving for a better place, and yet she probably also knew it would be full of challenges, disappointments, successes, sadness, and hard work, as she had already experienced. For me this girl embodied kindness, spunk, and humility.

When she came to my house to say good-bye, we sat next door on a low garden wall. My friend said, *"De recuerdo,"** and opened her hands and gave me five rubber hair rolls, the type that had a clip that you flipped in place once you rolled your hair. That simple and humble gift was all that she had to give as a memento of her and of Cuba. Such things were irreplaceable in Cuba. She would not be able to buy more.

It was like the widow's mite of a donation that Jesus saw as so valuable because it was all that she could give and more than she could afford. My friend didn't say, "Don't forget me." She didn't have to. I never did and I never will. She was a noble soul.

---

* As a memento.

Looking back, I realize that very often in life we meet a person who touches us in an unforgettable manner. We may have close and long-time friends who do unforgettable things for us too, like our neighbor two houses down. When she learned we had no food, she ran back to her house and scraped the remaining ends of two *plátanos**—all she had to eat—to give to my little nephew. Yet just as often, our dearest friends and the people we remember for the rest of our lives are people we encounter only once or twice. I am talking about kind strangers who act as friends to us, like the *campesino* who sold my father a chicken because he knew his family was hungry, even though our money was near worthless; the jail guard who stood his ground and made sure my father stayed in section one; some of the government officials my mother and I visited, who were likely responsible for my father receiving a lighter sentence and being transferred to the work farm; or the ballet school instructor next to the Teatro Infante, who did not want to hurt my mother and so told her kindly that there were no openings in the school instead of telling her that she was not allowed to enroll the sons and daughters of those who were leaving Cuba.

One of my best friends was the sweet girl who gave me five irreplaceable hair rollers—something you can pick up for a dollar in the United States, but which she would never be able to replace in Cuba. Though she was just a school acquaintance, she made sure she came to say good-bye and gave the only thing she had, without asking for anything in return.

We never know when Christ will be right in front of us.

---

* Plantain.

La Despedida (The Farewell)

From this point on, everything was a blur. On April 16, we left our house and went to my grandmother's. I remember that a few pieces of our clothing were strewn over the bed in her spare bedroom to be packed.

We spent our last night in our hometown in my grandmother's house. My mother's family on both sides was huge. She had many uncles, aunts, and cousins. Family and more family kept coming over to bid us farewell. Our friends from all over Holguín and the surrounding vicinity also came to say good-bye.

Finally, it was time to say the final good-bye. My grandmother was sitting in her rocking chair right in the middle of the dining room. I looked at her and saw tears streaming down her cheeks. Her tears were so clear I could see every detail of her skin beneath. She was about to be ripped apart from her youngest child—whose soul was interwoven with hers—forever.

"Grandmother, don't cry," I told her.

As I was standing there with her, I watched my oldest aunt walk into Grandma's bedroom to give a good-bye kiss to my nephew, who was sleeping on the bed. I decided not to follow her. It was her private moment. She would never see us again.

Then I watched my mother with her mother. They were hugging in an embrace that did not want to let go, an embrace that seemed to say, "This is not happening." Then I realized that my mom and her family had never really sat down and discussed that our leaving was for real, that our good-byes could be forever. For them, there had always been the tiniest hope that Fidel would be brought down and things would go back to the way they were, when families could stay together.

Everything else is a blur. I am sure I kissed them all good-bye; I am sure I hugged them all good-bye.

My father walked over to get my mother and slowly, but persuasively, began to guide her out of the house. She was shaking her head back and forth in despair and disbelief. It was clear that my mother did not want to leave her mother.

My mother feared for her family, leaving them in Cuba. She was not wrong about the catastrophes to come. As it happened, in addition to their emotional suffering, her family suffered horrible events. My grandmother had taken in two boarders about a year before we left, about whom my mother had an uneasy feeling. In fact, they took advantage of my grandmother. While my aunt was hospitalized, poisoned by a mysterious toxin from which she ultimately died, the boarders tricked my grandmother into signing the *traspatio* over to them. The disturbing news of this fraud, of the terrible death my aunt suffered from the poison, and of the progressively worsening conditions under which her family lived overwhelmed my mother and eroded her mental health, as it was added to the stress of leaving her family and homeland and acclimatizing to a new culture. Had my mother been able to bring all of her family over to the States, perhaps her depression would not have taken over. Instead, once we came to the States, bouts with depression and insomnia were frequent.

Yet, even with the ups and downs we went through after arriving in the United States, she worked for fifteen years. Sometimes I wondered how she could get up and go to work each day. In her last years, she succumbed to Alzheimer's, which robbed her of her beautiful handwriting, her mind, and her memory, except for distant memories of her mother, her siblings, and Cuba. That part of her mind remained clear almost until the end.

She would say, "Mi *Cubita*, mi *Cubita*,[*] how I loved you and how I lost you."

Toward the end, she would ask, "My sisters suffered a lot before they died, eh?"

I would lie and answer her, "No, Mami; they were old and so they died, but they did not suffer."

She would say, "Oh, I thought they had suffered," but my answer would soothe that part of her memory that still lived.

Yet as we were leaving that day, as my father put his hands on my mother's shoulders and walked behind her, gently moving her forward, I saw his face. It was full of joy in anticipation of our new life.

Our neighbor Manuel was the only one on our street who still had a working car, so he took us to the bus station in Holguín. Manuel and his family were not Fidelistas, but they could not leave Cuba because they had sons, all military age. They would stay and keep the family together.

We spent most of the night at the bus station until our bus took off from Holguín sometime after midnight. My Grandmother Cuca stayed with us and saw us off. My sister, her ex-husband, my little nephew, his godfather, and I left on the first bus for Varadero. My father, my mother, and my nephew's paternal grandmother stayed behind for the next bus. They were waiting for my grandfather Victor, my father's father, who

---

* My little Cuba, my little Cuba (an affectionate diminutive).

barely made it to the bus station to say good-bye to his first-born son.

My mother told me later that my father had a window seat on the driver's side of the bus. He and his father clasped hands through the open window. My grandfather would not let go of my father's hand. The bus began to move forward slowly. My grandfather kept walking along with the bus, holding his son's hand. He'd already been forced to say good-bye to his daughter and his son, and he couldn't let go. The bus driver had a good heart. He pulled out of the station very slowly to give father and son a few more seconds. I am sure, if he is alive today, he has never forgotten that moment or the heart-wrenching stories about the thousands of Cubans he drove to Varadero between 1965 and the early 1970s.

The bus picked up speed and my grandfather broke into a little run to keep up, and then he had to let go. He would never see his son again. He died before receiving *el telegrama*.

I ask you, the reader, to imagine an elderly man running beside a departing bus, saying good-bye to a son he would never see again because of a rigid political ideology. Imagine how his head and shoulders bowed when he could no longer keep up and the burden of the loss settled down on him. Imagine his son tearing his eyes away and facing forward with a lump in his throat.

Some Cubans kissed the ground or knelt in grateful prayers when the Freedom Flights delivered them to Miami. Yet mingled with the joy of freedom and escape there was also the sorrow of leaving family, friends, and homeland behind. Such things were not meant to be. People should not have to endure this, not because of a political system.

There were many happy family reunions through the Freedom Flights too, when relatives who had been left behind finally received their telegrams. They were met at the airport by their relatives and embraced into their new country by warm, welcoming, familiar arms.

The bus ride to our departure point in Varadero was arranged by the government. At the beginning of the Freedom Flights, there were all kinds of rumors, including one that people who were emigrating had to sleep in Varadero's parks. I don't know if this was true at one time, but we stayed the first night in a house that had seasonal vacation accommodations.

We spent one day on the most beautiful beach in the world, our Cuban beach. Everything was moving so fast that I was not really present, so I could not fully appreciate it. I do remember that my nephew, who was one and a half, amused himself covering my hair with sand. I remember, too, that my sister and I went to the shoreline. She wore three simple silver bracelets symbolizing her birth month, March—which she had declared for customs. We were in shallow water, and she felt something in the water that scared her. She began to run toward the shore. I panicked and grabbed her arm, and the three silver bracelets slipped from her wrist. Before I could catch them, the ocean swallowed them up.

We spent the late afternoon, evening, and night of April 19th at the Veradero airport in an area designated for those who were leaving on the following morning's Freedom Flight. No others could enter. Any farewells had to be said at the entrance to the restricted area, so we said good-bye to my nephew's father, grandmother, and godfather and passed through the gate.

Everything was so emotionally charged that I don't remember much. I do remember people asking one another, "Where are you from?" and hearing that the departing families were from all over the island. Different people showed different emotions, but there was little joy. Some were crying or showed signs of having cried. People's hands trembled, and everyone was quiet. Even the children were very quiet. In the late afternoon, Cuban officials called each of our names and checked our visas. When one name was called out, there was no answer. Then I heard a woman say that her relative had renounced his visa. She was crying.

No one slept. We all just sat there through the night. There was kind of a feeling that said, *We are here. This is final.*

Morning came. Everyone was served creamy, homemade hot chocolate. It tasted so good to me. I had not had anything so delicious in a very long time. How ironic that a Cuban had to be leaving the country to get something decent to eat! At ten o'clock, U.S. immigration officers, who appeared to have flown in on the plane, called us one at a time and looked at our visas and passports. One by one, we silently boarded the plane.

Outside, our family watched from afar as our Freedom Flight took off on April 20, 1970. The relatives of those who were on the flight and other Cubans who were just enjoying the sand and water stood on the beach and looked up. When we were right over their heads, on our way to liberty, they threw up their arms and cheered.

* * *

A baby must be terrified as he hears the burst of the floodwaters when the womb is emptied of the warm water he has been suspended in since his conception. It must seem like the end of the world, and it is: is it the end of his world as he knows it.

He comes down the birth canal in the roiling embrace of heaving red walls and wet muscles strained to their utmost. His tiny brain receives neurological impulses of great pain, stress, and fear from the person who has protected him for so long. He hears the muffled thunder of his mother's screams reverberating in his tiny eardrums through the walls of muscle and bone. A baby's skull is compressed just in time, the bones sliding over one another, so the head can fit through a frighteningly narrow opening. The baby's helpless, naked, dependent body is then propelled through an earthquake of flesh that both embraces and threatens to crush him.

It must feel like death. Birth and death are not so very different, perhaps, as we leave the embrace of bones and flesh and are expelled into a life unknown.

I think we felt a little like that on the Freedom Flight to Miami. There was some death and some birth as we left Cuba, the mother's womb that had held our family for so long. There was heaving and upheaval and outcries of pain as our old world contracted around us and ejected us into a new one.

Yet it was a new birth, a new life, breathing the pure oxygen of freedom instead of the stifling, lifeless, gray sludge water of Castro's Cuba. We were reborn out of death.

Cuba was not so lucky.

Cuba's revolution once seemed to be a new birth of freedom, heralded by one of the headiest and most exciting victory parades in human history and achieved by a remarkably unified national will. Yet what appeared to be a birth was actually the death of the republic. Instead of being nurtured, the infant republic of freedom was systematically starved after it emerged from the womb—until it was no more.

Thoughtful Cubans must look backward to find national happiness and their true identity as a people—back to life before Fidel, as a very old person must look backward to memories for happiness. We have experienced, in full, the death of our republic.

Will there be rebirth for Cuba? I hope so. Maybe there are enough remnants of the Cuban soul, even among the doctrinaire communist youth who know no other Cuba but Fidel's that someday Cuba will shine again as the Pearl of the Caribbean.

Such paradoxes exist. As Saint Francis said, it is through death that we come into eternal life.

Cuba libre.

Epilogue[*]

Sometimes, when I dream of Cuba I find myself walking on the far right corridor of shops around Calixto García Park or on Calle Martí, walking away from the park in the direction of home. It is always very crowded in my dream. It is alive and full of life. But it's just a dream.

Night reached its peak blackness in Cuba a decade and a half ago. Today, while there are a few glimmers of light, darkness still prevails. The Stalinist-style Castro dictatorship that has ruled Cuba for over half a century has reached its full cycle and has taken its inevitable and predictable toll of destruction at all levels.

Cuba is bankrupt. The final crumbling of the Cuban communist regime is now obvious even to those who swore by it, including Fidel. Cuba cannot support itself. Without the country's knowledgeable cane growers, who were ousted by Fidel's collectivism, Cuba's sugar cane production declined to 1.2 million tons in the 2010–2011 harvest.[42] To place this in perspective, Cuba's production ran from 4–7 million tons throughout the 1950s.[43] When the Soviet Union dissolved in 1991, taking its multi–billion-dollar subsidies out of Cuba, the island turned to Europe for tourist income and Venezuela for aid to help support its economy; it worked for a little while. However, by 2005 with the worsening world economy the bottom began to fall out of

---

[*] Unless otherwise cited, information in this epilogue was obtained from relatives and friends who remained in Cuba and from Cuban friends who have returned to visit.

Cuban tourism. Additionally, Cuba's 2004 decision to raise the value of their currency by 20 percent made Cuba less of a vacation bargain.[44] For almost two decades, Cuba was almost totally dependent for aid and oil on Hugo Chávez, Venezuela's communist president and Fidel's disciple. It is hard to know how long Chávez's successor will continue to prop up Fidel and his brother, Raúl.

Cuba no longer has a job for everyone. Many employees who worked in tourism have been let go. Recently with travel restrictions eased, tourism has increased, but it is not enough to prop up the Cuban economy. Thousands of other government employees (nearly all Cubans are government employees) face the possibility of layoffs. The average Cuban salary for those who do have employment is the equivalent of twenty dollars a month.[45] This meager salary is paid mostly in Cuban pesos, which can only be used for a limited range of foods and basic goods.

Private enterprise is very limited, despite the government having sold licenses for possible future businesses. Many Cubans with a dream have obtained a license, but most have been unable to pursue their dreams further because there is no capital to borrow and no way for them to earn and save the money that they need to get a business off the ground. Additionally, Cuba's economy is too weak to provide a broad consumer base or to supply sufficient goods to keep a business going. Frequent harassment by government inspectors, often accompanied by exorbitant fines, further impedes success.

Another obstacle to economic recovery is Cuba's dual monetary system, which fosters a strong black market economy and an economically apartheid society. In 2004, Fidel prohibited direct use of the U.S. dollar in Cuba and established a second monetary system: the convertible peso, sometimes referred to as the "dollar," which in Cuba is worth roughly the same as the U.S. dollar and *twenty-five times more* than the Cuban peso. Tourists and Cubans who get American currency from their families in the States must exchange U.S. dollars for convertible pesos. The convertible peso does not, however, have value outside of Cuba.[46] It's ironic that a republic whose currency before Fidel was on a par with the American dollar has come to this.

Urban hunger is even more severe than when I left Cuba in 1970. There is no consistent transport of produce from farms to cities. Food production, like sugar cane production, declined dramatically with the collectivization of farms. Further, most of the food produced in Cuba never reaches general distribution, where it could be purchased with Cuban pesos. Instead, it is sold on the black market for American dollars or convertible pesos. Shops that sell the kinds of fruits and vegetables that the government has deemed "essential" must trade in national pesos. It's many a day that a Cuban does not eat because he doesn't have a "dollar." Dollar shops, which sell "nonessential" foods and other goods when available generally take only convertible pesos.[47]

When looking at a crowd of Cubans, you can see who has access to dollars by their better-fed appearance and their dress. A wide chasm lies between the well-being of Cuban farmers and urban Cubans. Unlike their urban countrymen, *campesinos* generally have plenty of food. And with the American dollars that they get on the black market, they can buy whatever is available in dollar-only stores.

If you have an American dollar in Cuba, you are the new rich.

Cuba's communist system has left its mark on nearly every person. Cubans have been gradually and systematically deprived of the comforts usually afforded by diligent work. A hard life characterized by scarce food; bad nutrition; and lack of medical, dental, and optical care has altered the way most Cubans look, speak, think, dress, and even walk, making them unrecognizable compared to their former selves. When I dare to go on the Internet to look at current photos and videos of Holguín and other parts of Cuba, I don't recognize my fellow Cubans.

Because most Cubans have no money to buy umbrellas and hats, a people who always took measures to protect themselves from the hottest of the sun's harmful rays, they look out from wrinkled, leathery, and often toothless faces. A proud people, who would shine their shoes before going anywhere, are shoeless or in flip-flops. A people who nearly universally took care with their appearance whenever they went out may now be found sitting shirtless on a curb.

Hunger and necessity can change people spiritually as well. Just walk through any Cuban city today. Houses whose front doors were ajar from morning until dusk are now screened with barbed wire and chain-link fences as people try to protect themselves and their belongings, especially their food. People desperate to feed their families—people who would never have in the past—become thieves, for the system pushes them to the limit.

Cuba is stuck in time. The nation's infrastructure has largely fallen into decay. The republic that had excellent railway and highway systems is literally back to mass truck transportation and the horse and buggy. It is not unusual to see a picture of beat-up, horse-drawn taxi carriages waiting outside Lenin Hospital in Holguín. Held together with whatever can be found, they are bits and pieces of a time gone by. The Carretera Central retains its structural integrity, but otherwise many roads and streets are crumbling, in some cases beyond repair. City streets are dirty, and houses are rundown and dilapidated. Weather and lack of care have erased the names from tombstones.

Evidence of the misery that has settled on Cuba is apparent in a new exodus. Professionals are still kept out of private practice and continue to be government employees. The smartest of them leave Cuba when they can. Some come to the States to visit family and ask for asylum. Others who are sent abroad on various government missions try to escape to the States. To stem the tide of defecting physicians, the government has taken possession of doctors' diplomas. Cuban blacks, who were excluded from Fidel's government for decades while being used as pawns in propaganda and as state trophies in the Olympics and the Pan American games, are also defecting. Ironically, the Judas Goat and the Bay of Pigs mole—betrayers of their own people—have also abandoned Fidel's Cuba and emigrated to the United States. Even Fidel's pride and joy, los Jóvenes Comunistas, and his "everyone-is-literate" people are leaving him. Many of them, having been brainwashed since birth, come to the United States with anti-American sentiments, yet the United States is their first choice of destination.

Cubans are still very much in the dark about what is happening in the world. Ninety-nine percent literacy in Cuba does not equate to a well-informed or well-educated citizenry. Not long ago I read about a tourist who was astounded when a Cuban hotel worker asked to see a map of the United States on the tourist's laptop. The hotel worker had never seen such a map.

Only a very small percentage of regular Cubans have cell phones, and the use of the phones is regulated by the government. Most Cubans do not have access to the Internet. News of uprisings in the Middle East and economic riots in Europe, which could stir unrest, are kept from the Cuban people. Only Fidel, Raúl, and other high government officials have knowledge of world events that are widely reported throughout the rest of the world. And, even if they had freedom to obtain them, Cubans couldn't afford computers, cell phones, or an Internet connection.

Any movement to depose Fidel and Raúl's regime would require arms and high-tech communication, including social media. Cuba's being an island makes smuggling weapons into the country literally impossible, and high tech won't come to Cuba until the Castro brothers are gone. These two have always guarded their lives well.

Fidel Castro, the charismatic bearded hero, the man whom everyone wanted to interview, and whom interviewers called fascinating, now seems to be nothing more than a decayed husk of another era. Clad in a jogging suit, no longer wearing his olive green fatigues, Fidel, the man who would spend hours in full-tilt tirades against the United States, is helped by an aide and sends messages to the people saying he cannot participate in government-orchestrated parades.

However, it does not matter that Fidel is aging. It is the character of the system that Fidel Castro brought to Cuba more than fifty years ago that continues to inflict misery on the majority of most Cubans.

In 2010, an *Atlantic* magazine journalist reported that Fidel had confided, "The Cuban model doesn't even work for us anymore."[48] More telling, over the past few years, American newspapers have reported Raúl Castro as saying, "The country is paying the price for errors made in the past," and, "Maybe we made a mistake."[49] Yet, never have they admitted—and never will they admit—that the system never worked, that *communism* doesn't work. They have not admitted that they sold out Cuba to the Soviet Union. Never has there been a true admission of responsibility for destroying Cuban society and Cuban prosperity with the imposition of communism. Instead, their feeble statements seem to me to be a cry for help.

Yet, Fidel and Raúl continue to try to impress the world with charades. From Elian Gonzalez to Ebola, Fidel has never missed an opportunity to aggrandize himself and to manipulate world opinion. Most recently, Fidel and Raúl sent Cuban physicians to serve in the Ebola outbreak in Africa. Less known is that these physicians will not be allowed reentry into Cuba if they become infected with Ebola, because Cuban health care remains inferior and Cuba doesn't even have a handle on other infectious diseases, such as cholera, let alone the ability to respond to a new lethal disease.

Due to Fidel's ailments, Raúl has been at Cuba's helm since 2006, first informally performing the role of First Secretary of Cuba's communist party in his brother's place, and then formally assuming the position in February 2008. In 2011, delegates of the Sixth Congress of the Communist Party of Cuba, who no doubt wished to keep their heads attached to their necks, elected Raúl president of Cuba.

Raúl does not seem to have any idea about how to resolve the economic situation in Cuba. He continues to pander to Venezuela, showing up every time there is a ceremony to honor the deceased Hugo Chávez, so that President Maduro, who persists in leading his country down Cuba's path, will continue to provide aid. Raúl has not opened the door to knowledgeable economists who have helped other Latin American countries grow their economies. There is little to ration, and there are hints that the *libreta* may be at risk of being eliminated, despite its being the primary source of food and goods for many in the nation. Raúl has been quoted in American newspapers as saying the *libreta* is "an unbearable weight on the economy" [50] along with pitiful statements such as, "We must live within our means" and "Two plus two is four, never five, much less six or seven."[51]

Among his unsuccessful attempts to fix the economy, Raúl has tried to increase food production by leasing farmland—land Fidel stole from Cuban farmers—to foreign farming companies. The government now also leases some land to small Cuban farmers, who are supposed to sell their produce in Cuban cities, but there is much corruption, and as noted, most of the food ends up being sold on the black market.

Fidel and Raúl admit that the economic situation on the island is dire, but they allow change only on their terms without giving up any power, which could open the door for an uprising or coup that could cost them their lives. Younger politicians who could have provided new talent have not been tapped for top cabinet positions. Instead, Cuba's leadership council continues to be dominated by the old party wolves. In late 2012, Raúl did suggest term limits to make way for new leadership. Even then, the limits proposed would allow him to stay in office until 2019, when he will have reached the age of eighty-eight.[52]*

Then there is the U. S. embargo.

The crowd that wants the embargo lifted has a good point—it's been more than fifty years, and the Cuban people are suffering. The embargo has not changed the political system in Cuba. Cuba and Cubans need to move forward, and the embargo is one element standing in the way of the country's recovery.

The crowd that does not want the embargo lifted until Fidel faces justice also has a good point, but they need to remember that, sadly, there is no justice for communist dictators. Stalin alone executed at least 20 million people and worked to death or starved another 40 million. Communist governments of the twentieth century, Fidel's included, are responsible for killing more than 140 million people.[53] Fidel and Raúl will never be put on trial for their atrocities, and Fidel has also gotten a pass in public opinion. Not even Nelson Mandela, who experienced long-term political imprisonment, called Fidel on his kangaroo courts or his government's gross mistreatment of thousands of unjustifiably incarcerated Cubans. Fidel will soon face God on his judgment day, but there will be no justice on earth.

---

* In 2013, Raúl announced that he would retire in 2018, one year before the new term limits require.

Life is and will continue to be unbearably hard for the Cuban people, from the minute they get up to the minute they lie down. Yet, in this dark landscape, some changes for the better have occurred in recent years. Up to a point, if they do not speak against the government, Cubans are now allowed to talk to one another about shortages and the economic situation without fear of being jailed. Border patrol laws have been relaxed; the government no longer shoots the thousands who try to escape Cuba on rafts (fewer mouths to feed). Travel restrictions and issuance of visas have been loosened, and each year tens of thousands of people are using emigration and tourist visas to move to the United States.[54]

The Catholic Church has managed to open dialog with the Cuban government, and it has had some success in quietly working for the release of a number of political prisoners. The church is allowed to print church-related material, but the clergy must still be very careful as to what they say. Most recently, the church has been able to speak out about the extreme poverty in Cuba. Especially since Pope John Paul II's visit to Cuba in 1998, Cubans have had more religious freedoms that allow them to attend church without fear and to hold outdoor religious processions. Nonetheless, the number of people who go to church is very small compared to before Fidel's takeover in 1959. After years of youth indoctrination by an atheist state, faith will have to be rebuilt.

When I search for the Cuba of my childhood, some traces remain. The rail-less stairway to the bell tower at San Isidoro is still there. Father Peña, who baptized me, who served my First Communion, and who confirmed me, became Holguín's first bishop and is now a retired monsignor living in Holguín. Although the house numbers have changed, the houses my grandfather built on Calle Fomento and Calle Cervantes are still there; some in better shape than others, some totally altered.

Only one family from the old days remains on our block. Some left; others died. In another few decades, there will be no one to remember the character of our street or of Cuba before Castro. On Calle Frexes, there is an archive of photographic negatives from the former Studios Sueiro and Casals. Although there is no money to organize them, in these photos is the history of Holguín, City of Parks, and a history of the families who built Holguín; a history that could inform Cuban children of their cultural heritage and of what Cuba looked like before Fidel came to power.

What will happen in Cuba after the Castro brothers are gone? It's hard to tell. Things will get worse before they get better; that is a given. I could be wrong, but I don't think there will be a revolution. The foreign news cameras will come in just like they did in Russia and Eastern Europe after the collapse of the Soviet Union. They will show a minimal reality of what life is like under a communist dictatorship. Their reports will soon be forgotten.

Despite the truth and a great deal of evidence to the contrary, it is likely that Fidel Castro and Che Guevara will always be heroes to the uninformed, to those who won't seek out the truth, and to those who know the truth but are totally devoted to their dogma. Many speculate that Fidel is near death. If Fidel's burial place is divulged, it will be interesting to see how his fellow Cubans respond to it. I do know that it is likely to become a shrine for living and unborn radicals who are willing to do anything to obtain their goals. The tentacles of Karl Marx and 1917 will ensnare other unbalanced minds and perhaps strangle another people.

Nonetheless, in a limited way, I am optimistic about Cuba's future, especially now that the United States and Cuba have normalized diplomatic relations. Already more and more visitors will be drawn to the once romantic city of Havana, cruise ships have already docked in Cuban ports, daily ferries will run from Florida, and tourists from all over the world will once again bring their vehicles and hop on the Carretera Central.

I am also realistic about Cuba. The United States had Cuba on the list of governments that sponsor terrorism, but Cuba was recently removed from this list as part of negotiations to reestablish relations.[55] Cuba's position in the gulf with its proximity to the United States makes it a perfect target for something very dark and very evil to engulf it, all in the name of hatred for the United States. This danger remains.

As for me, spending my early years in communist Cuba has molded me in many ways. Foremost, it made me strong. I am a survivor. I learned at an early age to think for myself and to hold my head up and not be too concerned about what others think of me. Beyond that, I still shut off the faucet when I brush my teeth and won't water the grass. No matter how small the dinner leftovers are, I save them for lunch. I am both frugal and extravagant. I save, but if I want something special, I get it, for I know life can change in the blink of an eye. I can interpret body language, understand broken English regardless of the nationality of the speaker, and pretty much figure out where foreigners are from. I am very observant and can tell what is going on in a room without letting it be known that I am watching. I am slow to divulge information, especially if someone is asking questions. I quickly spot propaganda and indoctrination, and I am leery of liberals and their leftist cousins because there is an aspect of Marxism in their beliefs, whether they know it or not.

I have come to terms with the fact that, by and large, the world does not know that Castro's military support of communist movements in Africa and Latin America have contributed to the destabilization of functional societies, tearing families apart and causing tens of thousands, perhaps hundreds of thousands, of deaths. I have come to understand and accept that those who still love or admire Castro, some of whom even think that Cuba got what it deserved, share two common denominators: a belief in some ideal or dogma related to Marxism and a hatred of the United States. I also have come to terms with the fact that Castro and the Cuban people will never be widely understood and accurately judged. I have accepted that unless you have lived the Cuban Revolution, you can't grasp the experience. It is just not possible. You can imagine it, but you cannot truly comprehend it.

I heard someone say—I don't know who—that when people lose their liberty, any future liberty they attain will never be the same. I think this is true. Cuba may be free again, and perhaps it will return to being a constitutional republic, but it will never be the same Cuba. Even if Cuba recovers financially, it will not be the same society. It is going to take time for people's lives and the standard of living to improve. Even then, there will be a new rich, and the gap between poor and rich will be much wider than before Fidel. Even if Cuba opens up entirely and children of Cuban refugees return to live in Cuba, they will never know it. It will never again be the pre-1959 Cuba. The lives of those who left, the lives of those who stayed, and the lives of their children and their children's children have been changed forever.

Che Guevara may become just a face on a faded T-shirt, but Fidel Castro will live on. It is certain that historians won't be able to talk about the twentieth century without talking about Fidel Castro. Throughout history, he will be resurrected again and again; and that, which is, I think, what he wanted.

Certainly Fidel Castro's shadow has and will darken Cuba for a long time to come, leaving scars on the country's altered soul.

Acknowledgments

There are so many to thank—the list is endless. I will be forever grateful to each and every one of you, who at different times in my life, perhaps without knowing it, have contributed to my ability to write this Cuban memoir.

I am grateful to my husband, Tony, who, by suggesting that I work part-time rather than full-time so I could be a hockey mom, gave me more time to work on my manuscript. A heartfelt thank-you to family and friends for their prayers and encouragement.

I would also like to extend my appreciation to Manuel González Beceña, son of the owners of Holguín's Grito de Yara department store. Many thanks to the University of Rochester's Miner Library research staff, whose guidance has been invaluable; to Dr. Eric Baklanoff, research professor emeritus of economics at University of Alabama, for his generous response to my inquiries; and a special thanks to my eighth-grade school counselor, Alberto Martínez, a *paisano*, who helped me get out of a terrible school system and set my feet on greener pastures. It would take many years for me to realize what a positive change he made in my life. Thank you for your great act of kindness, Mr. Martínez. You and your family are in my prayers always. And thank you to Sister Mary Bryan, former school principal at Our Lady of Mercy High School. A shout-out to Kay Derochie for book cover input and for always being there to answer my questions.

Above all I am grateful to my entire family, especially my mother, for passing on so much information to me and for capturing our family history in photos before Fidel Castro's regime changed everything.

Endnotes

1. Jaime Suchlicki, *Cuba from Columbus to Castro and Beyond*, 5th ed. (Dulles, Virginia: Brussey's, 2002), 38.

2. Ibid., 40.

3. International Labor Organization of Geneva, Switzerland, 1960, cited in "Cuba before Fidel Castro," trans. Gladys P. Martínez, (Burbank: *Contacto Magazine*). http://www2.fiu.edu/~fcf/cubaprecastro21698.html.

4. Calixto C. Masó, *Historia de Cuba*, ed. Leonel-Antonio de la Cuertas, 3rd ed. (Miami: Ediciones Universal, 1998), 710.

5. Eric N. Baklanof, "Cuba on the Eve of the Socialist Transition: A Reassessment of the Backwardsness-Stagnation Thesis," Cuba in Transition, Vol. 8 (Washington D.C., Association for the Study of the Cuban Economy, 1998), 264-265.

6. Archives of the Cuban Labor Ministry, cited in "Cuba Before Fidel Castro," trans. Gladys P. Martínez, *Contacto Magazine*, http://www2.fiu.edu/~fcf/cubaprecastro21698.html.

7. Masó, *Historia de Cuba*, 647.

8. Archives of the Cuban Labor Ministry, cited in "Cuba Before Fidel Castro," trans. Gladys P. Martínez, *Contacto Magazine*, http://www2.fiu.edu/~fcf/cubaprecastro21698.html.

9. Opinion expressed by some of my Cuban acquaintances who are a generation older than I, and also expressed by Masó in *Historia de Cuba*, 665.

10. Georgie Anne Geyer, *Guerrilla Prince*(Kansas City: Prince Andres McMeel,1991), 40.

11. Ibid., 50–51.

12. Ibid., 42.

13. Huber Matos, *Como Llegó la Noche* (Barcelona: Tusquets Editores, 2002), 176–77.

14. Masó, *Historia de Cuba*, 668.

15. Ibid, 669.

16. Geyer, *Guerilla Prince*, 158–59.

17. Matos, *Como Llegó la Noche*, 127.

18. Masó, *Historia de Cuba*, 694.

19. Ibid, 675.

20. Masó, *Historia de Cuba*, 286–287.

21. José M Illán, *Cuba: Facts and Figures of an Economy in Ruins*, trans George A Wehby (Miami, Editorial ATP, 1964), 96-99.

22. Masó, *Historia de Cuba*, 678.

23. "Cuba Before Fidel Castro," *Contacto Magazine*.

24. Masó, Historia de Cuba, 232.

25. Masó, *Historia de Cuba*, 678.

26. Fidel Castro, May 10, 1959, speech, Guines, Cuba.

27. Matos, *Como Llegó La Noche*, 314.

28. Masó, *Historia de Cuba*, 672.

29. Geyer, *Guerrilla Prince*, 231–32.

30. Masó, *Historia de Cuba*, 681.

31. Cuban Information Service, cited by Hugh Thomas, in *El Presidio Político en Cuba* (Caracas: ICOSOCV Ediciones, 1982), 194.

32. Masó, *Historia de Cuba*, 687.

33. Ibid, 687.

34. Ibid., 689.

35. Ibid, 687.

36. Ibid, 699.

37. Luisa Yanez, "Miami Herald Database Tracks Those Who Came on Freedom Flights," *Miami Herald*, November 16, 2008.

38. *El Presidio Político en Cuba Comunista: Testimonio* (Caracas: ICOSOCV Ediciones, 1982), and Matos, *Como Llegó la Noche*.

39. Geyer, *Guerrilla Prince*, 317.

40. World Health Organization, cited in "Cuba before Fidel Castro," *Contacto Magazine*," trans. Gladys P. Martínez, *Contacto Magazine*, http://www2.fiu.edu/~fcf/cubaprecastro21698.html.

41. Dr. Armando M. Lago and Charles J. Brown, *The Politics of Psychiatry in Revolutionary Cuba* (New Brunswick, New Jersey: Transaction Publishers, 1992), 12.

42. Arch Ritter, "Cuba Accepts Brazilian Investment in Its Most Emblematic Economic Sector: Sugar," *Reuters*, January 31, 2012. http://thecubaneconomy.com/articles/2012/01/cuba-

accepts-brazilian-investment-in-its-most-emblematic-economic-sector-sugar/.

43. Ilán, *Cuba: Facts and Figures*, 43.

44. Wilfredo Cancio Isla, "Cuban Tourist Economy in Trouble," *Miami Herald Online*, April 3, 2007, http://cubafile.blogspot.com/2007/04/cubas-tourist-economy-in-trouble.html.

45. Agence France-Presse, "Average Monthly Salary in Cuba Rises to $19," *MyFoxdc.com*, June 5, 2012, http://www.myfoxdc.com/story/18702466/average-cuban-monthly-salary-rises-to-19.

46. Wikipedia, "Cuban Convertible Peso," *Wikipedia*, accessed March 20, 2012, http://en.wikipedia.org/wiki/Cuban_convertible_peso.

47. Wikipedia, "Cuban Peso," *Wikipedia*, accessed March 20, 2012, http://en.wikipedia.org/wiki/Cuban_peso.

48. Jeffrey Goldberg, "Fidel: Cuban Model Doesn't Even Work for Us Anymore," *The Atlantic*, September 8, 2010, http://www.theatlantic.com/international/archive/2010/09/fidel-cuban-model-doesnt-even-work-for-us-anymore/62602/.

49. Peter Orsi, "Raúl Castro Proposes Political Term Limits in Cuba."*Herald Sun.* http://www.heraldsun.com/view/

full_story/12820722/article- Raúl Castro Proposes Political Term Limits in Cuba.

50. Shasta Darlington, "Castro Praises Brother Amid Historic Changes," *CNN*, April 17, 2011, http://www.afrocanada.net/index.php?option=com_content&view=article&id=12811 1:fidel-castro-praises-brothers-reforms&catid=1:latest&Ite mid=2.

51. Peter Orsi, "Raúl Castro Proposes Political Term Limits in Cuba," *Herald Sun*, http://www.heraldsun.com/view/full_story/12820722/article-Raul-Castro -proposes-political-term-limits-in-Cuba.

52. Ibid.

53. R. J. Rummel, "Statistics of Democide," *Death by Government* (New Brunswick, Transaction Publishers, 1994, updated online 1998), www.hawaii.edu/powerkills/NOTE/.htm.

54. "Cubans Flood U.S. after Travel Rules Ease," Associated Press, October 10, 2014.

55. http://www.state.gov/j/ct/list/c14151.htm;http://www.state.gov/j/ct/rls/crt/2010/170260.htm.

About Author

Author Photo by Lisa Mancini, HEartworks Photography

Dania Rosa Nasca was born in 1958 in Holguín, the City of Parks, Oriente, Cuba, the year the Cuban Revolution drove Batista from power.

She was given a front-row seat to Fidel Castro's takeover of the government and all private enterprise. When she was twelve, she and her family immigrated to the United States through a US-sponsored Freedom Flight.

She works as a financial counselor for the University of Rochester's Strong Memorial Hospital. She is active in her parish and closely follows world affairs, especially events in Cuba and other communist countries.

A proud Cuban American and a hockey mom who hates snow, she lives in Rochester, New York, with her husband, Tony, their son, Anthony, and their Chihuahua-Manchester terrier. Rochester has been her home ever since she arrived in the United States.

Made in the USA
San Bernardino, CA
25 August 2018